# The Profession of English
# in the Two-Year College

D0911721

## Also in the CrossCurrents series

# The Profession of English in the Two-Year College

Edited by

Mark Reynolds
and
Sylvia Holladay-Hicks

*New Perspectives in Rhetoric and Composition*

CHARLES I. SCHUSTER, SERIES EDITOR

Boynton/Cook Publishers, Inc.
HEINEMANN
Portsmouth, NH

**Boynton/Cook Publishers, Inc.**
A subsidiary of Reed Elsevier Inc.
361 Hanover Street
Portsmouth, NH 03801–3912
www.boyntoncook.com

*Offices and agents throughout the world*

**Library of Congress Cataloging-in-Publication Data**
The profession of English in the two year college / edited by Mark Reynolds, Sylvia
Holladay-Hicks.
    p. cm.
    Includes bibliographical references.
    ISBN 0-86709-579-2 (alk. paper)
    1. English philology—Study and teaching (Higher)—United States. 2. English
philology—Study and teaching—United States—History—20th century. 3. Community
colleges—United States. 4. English teachers—United States. 5. Junior colleges—United
States. I. Reynolds, Mark, [date]. II. Holladay, Sylvia A. III. Title.

PE68.U5P76 2005
428'.0071'173—dc22

                                 2004017512

*Editor: Charles I. Schuster*
*Production service: Merrill Peterson, Matrix Productions*
*Production coordinator: Elizabeth Valway*
*Cover design: Joni Doherty*
*Composition: Tom Allen/Pear Graphic Design*
*Manufacturing: Steve Bernier*

Printed in the United States of America on acid-free paper
09 08 07 06 05 VP 1 2 3 4 5

# Contents

# Preface

The two-year college is uniquely American: No other institution of higher learning is dedicated to fulfilling the educational needs and goals of *all* the people in a community. Teaching English in the two-year college is uniquely American: The instructors are committed to maintaining both excellence and egalitarianism in educational opportunity for *all* the people in a community. This book is uniquely American: It presents the origins and development of a new profession, the teaching of college English to *all* the people in a community.

This book had its origin in a conversation between Sylvia Holladay-Hicks and Audrey Roth at the 1997 NCTE Southeastern regional conference in Atlanta. After a day of speeches and workshops, they were discussing what had been accomplished in two-year-college English in the previous thirty years and reminiscing about previous meetings and colleagues—Dick Worthan, Liz McPherson, Harold Cummings, Dick Friedrich, Angela Harris, Don Tighe, Richard Williamson, Jim-El Harris, Bill Doster, and others. They wished that the new members of the regional group could talk with these friends and mentors to share the richness of their knowledge and fervor. One said, "Someone should write our history." The other added, "And in our own voices." They realized that most of the instructors of the 1960s had already retired or died, and the project took on a sense of urgency because they wanted to record as many early voices as possible. When these two talked to others at the convention, the others were enthusiastic about the proposed project. Mark Reynolds ran a call for papers in *Teaching English in the Two-Year College* and joined Sylvia in carrying the project through—contacting potential contributors; reading, editing, and selecting submissions; and searching for a publisher.

This book is the resulting story of some of those early instructors in two-year-college English, told in their own words. The collection grew out of the editors' conviction that a historical record of the early years would be valuable for the profession and for future instructors. We wanted this history to be written by those who faced and met the challenges of a new kind of education in this country. During the early years of the 1960s and 1970s, when the great growth in the number of two-year colleges occurred, there were no models for two-year English teachers, so they had to create themselves. They were challenged by new

vii

students, new demands, and new educational needs. Overall, they had—
and still have—the responsibility to help often ill-prepared students
improve their skills in writing and reading so that they could be successful in other college courses and in their chosen work. The instructors
quickly discovered that traditional techniques and materials did not work
with the new students, so they became flexible, adopted new attitudes,
and developed new methods that would work. Their dedication to their
students and to their profession is evident in this representative collection of voices.

We want to thank those who encouraged us in this project and all who
contributed to it. We appreciate all of those who submitted initial essays,
and we wish space had allowed us to include everyone. We especially
thank the ones who patiently stayed with us through several revisions.
We are grateful for those at Heinemann–Boynton/Cook who guided us
through the preparation of the final manuscript, especially acquisitions
editor Charles Schuster for his thoughtful editing and valuable suggestions. We especially appreciate the cogent and helpful suggestions of
reviewer Maureen Haurigan, Kent State University, Trumbull Campus.
Finally, we thank Karen Reynolds and Tom Hicks for their understanding and support of our professional activities through the years.

# Introduction

From 1960 through 1975, a new two-year college opened nearly every month. The colleges advertised their classes, and the students arrived in droves. Many colleges began classes in temporary facilities—churches, vacant commercial buildings, shopping centers, or abandoned schools—until permanent buildings could be constructed. In most cases, the general education course offerings followed the junior college model, duplicating the first two years of the state's major four-year institutions. Vocational or technical courses were added, usually modeled on those of area vo-tech high schools or based on quick surveys of area industries or chamber of commerce descriptions of area labor needs. The rapidity of the start-ups—locating facilities, hiring faculties, creating curricula, and recruiting students—was unprecedented in educational history.

In 1960, there were 582 community colleges, and in 1963, 590 (excluding branches) in the United States. By 1975, the number had almost doubled to 1,003 institutions (excluding branches). After that, the growth of new institutions continued more slowly, so that by 1994 there were 1,442 two-year college campuses (including branches) (*The Digest*, Table 236). During this same period, the enrollment in those colleges exploded: 1963—850,361; 1975—3,970,119, quadrupling in just 12 years; 1994—5,529,710 (*The Digest*, Table 170).

The rapid and frantic beginnings of many institutions left little time for planning curricula, finding and hiring appropriate faculty, or studying the prospective student body or the educational needs of the surrounding community in depth. Consequently, during those early years both administrators and faculty found the unexpected at every turn. Of necessity, they employed innovative problem solving to meet the needs of a new kind of institution populated with a new breed of student needing a new model of English teaching. Truly, they were educational pioneers.

This book documents the evolution and development of two-year-college English teaching as a distinct and significant profession. Most of the accounts come from individuals with more than thirty years of teaching experience, and their stories record the history of those early boom years in the voices of those who lived it. The new types of students in the classrooms, curriculum such students needed, new institutions themselves, and communities where the colleges were located shaped this faculty. Collectively, these essays document the evolution of two-year-college English teaching into a mature and unique profession, one poised to take on the challenges of teaching English in a new century.

The essays in Part I chronicle how faculty responded to their new institutions and their students. Mark Reynolds leads off with an overview of how two-year-college faculty developed and grew as knowledge makers in the profession, particularly through curriculum material development, as they responded to their diverse students. In the next essays by Mary Slayter, Marilyn Smith Layton, and Richard Williamson, the authors describe how they came to their institutions and were themselves shaped by their new environments.

The essays in Part II describe how early faculty responded to the needs of students. First, Barbara Stout explains how she and her colleagues developed innovative and constantly changing writing programs. Next, William Costanzo focuses on his early use of film and computers. Dee Brock then details her career-long use of television in teaching. Finally, Alan Meyers explains the development of creative ESL programs to meet the needs of large immigrant populations.

Part III provides accounts of how faculty developed as professional teachers, individually and collectively, by Mary Sue Koeppel, Elizabeth Nist, Ann Laster, and Beverly Fatherree. Ellen Knodt then describes the history of formal graduate school faculty preparation and what is needed for the future. Howard Tinberg concludes this section with a bibliographic essay, selectively reviewing important studies of two-year-college English during this period and beyond.

As a whole, these essays help to provide a significant historical record of how individual faculty members responded to the phenomenal growth of two-year colleges, their highly diverse student populations, and their unique communities in order to lay the foundation for a new and different kind of professional—the two-year college teacher-scholar of English. As vast numbers of these pioneers move into retirement, these essays preserve their stories and chronicle first-hand what it was like to be at the forefront of the rapid growth and development of two-year institutions and their English faculties.

# Works Cited

*The Digest of Educational Statistics 1996*. Washington: GPO, 1996

# 1

## Two-Year-College Teachers as Knowledge Makers

### Mark Reynolds

## Introduction

Because of the nature and history of two-year institutions, their faculty did not routinely envision themselves as knowledge makers within the discipline of English studies. Two-year colleges have always concentrated on only the first two years of undergraduate education. In English, those years focus on developing the fundamentals of academic writing and reading, work usually relegated to graduate students in universities and often deemed by the academy as of lesser importance. In addition, two-year-college teachers have not seen themselves as specialists, researchers, or scholars in the classic sense. Because they teach nonspecialized courses at the introductory level of the discipline, their expertise is most often judged elementary or surface level, suitable for the nonspecialist, the generalist, or the less highly degreed. Many in the academy have also considered the two-year teacher's work as rudimentary rather than dealing with theory, abstract ideas, or formal research. Two-year-college teachers historically have been most concerned with pedagogy and praxis, with translating the complex into the simple for students, instead of discovering knowledge, defining new territory, or communicating complex ideas to peers.

Faculty members in the vast majority of two-year colleges have not had to conduct research or publish to get or keep a job. One exception has been faculty on two-year branch campuses of major state universities in states such as Ohio and Pennsylvania, where faculty have been held to the same tenure and promotion requirements as those on the universities' main campuses. The majority of two-year faculty members, however, unlike their university colleagues, were hired to teach, not to publish or create disciplinary scholarship. Two-year-college faculty members also work in institutions that admit any and all with a high school diploma or its equiv-

1

alent. Thus, these open-door institutions have often been viewed erroneously as having no standards. They are different, too, from much of higher education because comprehensive community colleges and two-year technical colleges place great emphasis on preparing students for the world of work after only a year or two of attendance. Most of the academy has not been able to relate to such utilitarian purposes, to training in skills such as automotive mechanics, computer drafting, nursing, cosmetology, air conditioning and refrigeration, welding, masonry, home health aid, postal management, and many other fields of employment.

In these institutions, some designated "junior," where the majority has had no system of professional or academic rank, faculty members have been commonly labeled "instructors." A concentrated effort throughout their history to avoid rank has resulted both from the strong emphasis placed on teaching and from the democratic spirit implicit throughout the two-year college's history and purpose for existing. As a result, those outside the institutions, especially those in universities, have tended to view two-year-college faculty merely as teachers, seldom as scholars or researchers. However, as Elizabeth Nist and Helon Raines have pointed out,

> Reasons exist for the predominance of two-year colleges naming all faculty "instructor," none of which has to do with value, ability, or education. Yet, "instructor" in university language designates the bottom of the academic hierarchy and connotes fewer degrees, less experience and/or ability, and minimal, if any scholarship or publication. (65)

For all of these reasons, then, the academy has seldom judged the two-year-college faculty member capable of making significant contributions to knowledge. Nor has it paid much attention to their efforts, judging them unworthy or insignificant. In fact, a national survey of faculty, conducted by The Carnegie Foundation for the Advancement of Teaching in 1997, dispels several stereotypes about community college faculty, including the one that they do not engage in or appreciate scholarly research. According to that report,

> The average difference in the amount of time that community college faculty and those of baccalaureate institutions spend each week performing research or comparable scholarly activities is only 2.3 hours. In addition, almost 80 percent of community college faculty engage in consulting or professional service." ("Casting" 45)

## History and Purposes

As indicated, much of the faculty role within two-year colleges has resulted from these institutions' historical origins and specialized functions. The most significant factor in their founding came from the efforts of some prominent university presidents to separate the first two years of college education from the last two. As early as the 1850s, several university presidents were calling for new institutions to take on the role of general education. Henry Tappan, president of the University of Michigan, William Rainey Harper, president of the University of Chicago, David Starr Jordan, president of Stanford University, and Alexis Lange, dean of the School of Education at the University of California, are usually given credit for encouraging such a split in the first decade of the twentieth century. Jordan, in particular, wanted to split the first two college years from the rest of the university in order to create a university more akin to its European ancestors, an elite institution focused on research and scholarship. He is credited with initiating the terms "junior" and "senior" colleges to refer to the two divisions. In 1901, two additional years were added to the high school in Joliet, Illinois, creating what has traditionally been labeled as the nation's first junior college (Cohen and Brawer 6–13).

Paralleling the division of universities into upper and lower strata, initiatives began in many separate localities in the country to create educational institutions of higher learning that responded to particular local needs and provided educational opportunities beyond high school to the less affluent. This response to the local communities in which they are located has been a hallmark of two-year colleges from their beginnings. Often, this response has been in the form of workforce preparation, preparing the local population as workers for a particular business or industry in the community. At other times, this function has meant addressing a significant area population with unique needs, especially by offering English as a Second Language programs to large immigrant populations. Community colleges in New York City, Chicago, Miami, and in parts of Texas and California offer examples of the latter. Responding to their local communities has always meant, as well, providing a variety of enrichment and leisure-time activities to area citizens (see Griffith and Connor for other descriptions of local response).

Since their founding in the early 1900s, two-year colleges have always sought to fill specific needs in American higher education beyond the traditional high school years. As a result, two-year institutions occupy an unusual position, lodged between the high school and the university, often seeming to belong to neither, and yet often integrally tied to both even though distinctly unlike either. As a result, these institutions have had to forge their own identity within their local environments, and they consider responses to local needs an important function.

Faculty have always been encouraged and, in some cases expected, to be involved in their communities. Colleges have traditionally tailored activities specifically to meet the needs of local constituencies, whether in the form of particular courses, workforce training, or cultural and enrichment programs. In English departments, such activities may have taken the form of computerized writing courses designed for a local industry, courses in technical or business writing, creative writing workshops at a community center, life writing courses at a retirement center, a discussion by a faculty member of Ebonics at a local civic club, or a topic such as "religion and literature" for a local religious group.

As a result of their open admissions policies, a major purpose of two-year colleges has been to provide training in basic skills to the large number of area students who enroll with deficiencies in language and mathematical skills. English departments have, therefore, created extensive programs of basic skills training—courses in remedial or developmental or basic writing and reading. In many colleges, these programs have several levels and include courses in study skills, orientation to college, library use, and either the incorporation of ESL courses within a basic skills program or the development of a separate ESL program, depending on local needs. In such programs, English teachers might work closely with counselors, learning skills specialists, librarians, speech teachers, specialists in learning disabilities, or occupational therapists.

According to Glen Gabert, it is the open admissions policy that "has been one of the most misunderstood characteristics of community colleges and has led to charges that they are second-rate institutions with low standards. It is more accurate to say that community colleges admit anyone who demonstrates reasonable potential for success in the program to which they seek admission" (15). Moreover, many separate programs, such as nursing, within institutions do have set admission requirements.

It has mainly been this basic skills function, often located within English departments on two-year campuses, with its heavy remedial emphasis, that has caused the academy to view two-year colleges as something less than collegiate, as more allied to the high school than the university, attending to a population that is not and never will be "college material." The remedial and vocational functions together cause some to consider two-year colleges both inappropriate and unworthy of being included within the higher education spectrum.

History shows, however, that the two-year college is the single most important element in what has been called the democratization of American higher education. That fact is self-evident when one observes the dramatic increase in the numbers of these institutions from the 1960s into the 1990s. At least one two-year college is located in every congressional district. Currently, over 1,400 public and private two-year colleges enroll over two million students full-time and an additional 3.6

million students part-time (*The ERIC Review* 25). Such numbers are impressive, considering the ever-increasing costs of higher education. Low costs alone have continued to attract students who, in the past, would only have attended a four-year college or university to the two-year college. According to statistics, approximately fifty percent of all students begin their higher education in two-year colleges (Doucette and Roueche 1). However, only about one-fifth of those continue their education by enrolling in the upper levels of colleges or universities.

Those who do, nevertheless, constitute a significant number, a number that will continue to increase with the rising costs of higher education. These are the students who fulfill the transfer mission of two-year colleges, completing the first two years of a four-year undergraduate education, equivalent to the first two years at most four-year colleges and universities. Significantly, studies consistently show that those transferring from two-year colleges to four-year colleges perform as well as or better than students who begin their work at the senior institution (see Gaskins, Holt, and Roeger).

It is also in fulfilling the transfer function that two-year colleges have been most like four-year colleges and universities. Two-year institutions offer both regular and advanced college composition, creative writing, and technical writing, a great variety of literature courses from traditional introductory courses to surveys of British and American literature, world literature, multicultural literature, and more specialized courses in women's literature, mystery, science fiction, and Native American and African American literature. In increasing numbers since their inception, two-year colleges have developed honors programs, and offer special honors courses to excellent students capable of high levels of performance in any educational setting.

## Faculty as Knowledge Makers

Because their primary concern has been teaching, two-year-college faculty members belong to that large body of practitioners who have contributed to what Stephen North has called lore, the knowledge that emanates from classrooms across the country and from teacher practice, much of which never gets written down but which circulates widely through practice and talk and, consequently, becomes knowledge.

Two-year-college faculty members traditionally have heavy teaching loads, three to six classes each term, and large numbers of students. Most of their teaching centers on composition and requires time-consuming paper reading. Such heavy workloads in and of themselves are major reasons so few two-year-college teachers have been active knowledge makers who have produced published accounts of their knowledge either through journal articles or book-length studies. Because of such workloads, many teachers have not felt connected to their discipline in formal ways. They cannot relate to the faculty who have the time, institutional support, and financial support for research, publication, or conference attendance and presentations. For years, many felt that what got published in the discipline's journals had little relevance to their daily work in the classroom.

However, with the establishment of the journals *Teaching English in the Two-Year College* (1974) and the *Journal of Basic Writing* (1978), two-year-college practitioners had places that welcomed their academic writing and knowledge making. These journals, in particular, have allowed two-year-college teachers to give reports of their work and have encouraged them to provide accounts of classroom practice. Indeed, with the establishment of a journal particularly for them, two-year-college English teachers have been much more prolific in their publishing efforts. Major journals in the discipline such as *College English* and *College Composition and Communication* have routinely published the work of two-year-college teachers and have kept one or more on their editorial boards and a number among their manuscript reviewers. These actions have encouraged and recognized the work of two-year-college English teachers and also provided incentives for their participation in the discipline's conversations.

Many two-year teachers have also produced textbooks that are repositories of their knowledge, many of them pioneering works and among the most widely used college texts. Pickett and Laster's technical writing textbook, which was the first on this subject at the introductory college level, is one of them. The first technical writing textbook by two-year-college teachers for two-year-college students, it is now in its eighth edition. (See Pickett, "A Quarter Century," for an account of the early travails two-year-college teachers faced getting textbooks published.) Audrey Roth's research manual, also in its eighth edition, grew from the author's experiences at Miami-Dade Community College and has been one of the most widely used guides at both two- and four-year institutions for introducing research methodology to beginning college students. The textbook by Elizabeth and Gregory Cowan, *Writing* (Wiley 1980), was one of the first and, perhaps, the most successful to incorporate the pedagogy of the process approach to writing. Both authors' experiences grew from their long years of teaching in two-year colleges. John Langan has had great success with his composition textbooks, especially those for basic writing and developmental reading. The composition texts and handbooks of Lynn Troyka and Diana Hacker have been among the most widely used in the nation's two- and four-year institutions. Hundreds of other two-year-college teachers have also written successful textbooks that convey their expertise on a variety of subjects. All of these texts are full of practitioner's lore, of knowledge useful to teachers. They represent the foundation of what is being taught throughout the first two years of college writing and reading in all institutions.

Another outlet for two-year teacher knowledge has been professional conferences. In 1965, the Conference on College Composition and Communication of the National Council of Teachers of English established seven regional conferences on English in the two-year college. Since that time, most of these regional conferences have conducted major professional meetings where two-year-college faculty have gathered to hear presentations about their teaching and professional concerns. The meetings have attracted nationally known scholars and such literary figures as Eudora Welty and James Dickey. The large numbers of attendees over the years and the long-standing success of these annual meetings attest to their value to two-year-college teachers and others (see Laster and Fatherree in this volume). These meetings have been major sites for teachers to pass on their knowledge. However, because the proceedings have not routinely been published, such knowledge too often has taken the form of North's lore.

Two-year-college teachers have also been active in all the major national professional organizations, giving papers at their meetings, serving on their committees, and often publishing in their journals. Their numbers have not been great, and their efforts most often have been individual ones; nonetheless, two-year-college participation has been long, regular, and constant, if not widespread, in NCTE, CCCC, MLA, ADE, CEA, the regional MLAs, and numerous regional and state professional organizations. This participation is even more remarkable when one remembers that many of these instructors work in institutions where research, scholarship, publishing, indeed knowledge making itself, is not valued. Two-year-college instructors have often engaged in these activities at their own expense and without institutional rewards. They do so for their personal intellectual stimulation and satisfaction, because they are serious scholars and researchers, and because they are motivated to contribute to the discipline's knowledge from their unique perspective. With the establishment of the Two-Year College English Association (TYCA) within the National Council of Teachers of English in 1996, and the Committee on Community Colleges within the Modern Language Association in 1997, opportunity for professional growth and development for two-year-college English faculty has expanded significantly.

## Kinds of Knowledge Two-Year-College Teachers Make

Two-year-college teachers are required in most institutions to have only a master's degree, although many do have Ph.D.s, D.A.s, and Ed.D.s.

While most faculty members do not view themselves as specialists in a narrow field within the discipline, they do consider themselves experts in the teaching of the first two college years of their discipline and in the craft of teaching itself. They more often consider themselves generalists, adaptable to students and settings and able to take complex materials and discover ways to communicate them effectively to varied audiences. It is in this teaching expertise that the academy might well learn most from two-year-college teachers. The majority long ago eschewed the lecture as the primary means of conveying material. They have long been knowledgeable about collaborative learning and the social construction of meaning. They long ago embraced the use of media in teaching, and they have been pioneers in the use of technology in the classroom (see Reynolds "Twenty-Five Years"; and *Teaching English in the Two-Year College* Special Issue).

They have also been pioneers in the development of writing centers, locales where they have addressed the needs not just of underprepared students, but also of students in all disciplines across their institutions. Howard Tinberg has published a monograph on the serious work that goes on in two-year-college writing centers. He makes a strong case that two-year-college faculty are experts in the dissemination of knowledge, more than in knowledge itself. His study demonstrates the strong commitment of a group of cross-disciplinary faculty to the teaching of writing to diverse students. Tinberg's work is an excellent example of the kinds of knowledge making two-year-college faculty have contributed and are capable of contributing to the discipline. Other examples of significant scholarly endeavors over the years by two-year English faculty include Paul Oehler's discography of American literature set to music, Jane Maher's biography of Mina Shaughnessy, Randy Cross' rescuing of T. S. Stribling's editions of long out-of-print Southern novels, and Karen Castelluci Cox's development of story cycle theory.

Because most two-year-college English departments are quite small, there has always been a good deal of cross-disciplinary interaction among the disciplines on two-year campuses, much more so than one usually finds at a university. It is not at all uncommon for faculty in English to combine for interdisciplinary work with faculty from mathematics, psychology, history, nursing, even automotive mechanics. Such work may take the form of team-teaching, of creating special courses for local businesses or industries, of collaboration for work with honors students, of campus committee work, writing center tutorials, or study skills labs. It is not uncommon for such faculty to meet and work together daily in environments that are integrated institutionally, providing a much more holistic and cohesive faculty than found on most four-year campuses. At some colleges, Santa Fe Community College in Gainesville, Florida, for example, faculty offices have not been organized by departments, but are interspersed campus-wide so that an English faculty member's office may be next door to a computer instructor's or a cosmetology instructor's. Such an arrangement makes for a more cohesive and integrated faculty community, one that encourages interdisciplinary solutions to campus problems and especially student learning.

It is probably in the teaching of nontraditional students that two-year-college teachers have produced the most valuable knowledge. Faculty members confront students who are first-generation college students for the most part—commuters, holders of part- and full-time jobs, with an average age of twenty-nine, and who view education often as a stop-in and stop-out event to be managed when their lives can accommodate a course or two: ". . . their lives zig and zag. They leave school to take a job or have a baby or reorganize their lives; they come back, perhaps with a different goal, a different attitude, once, twice, three times" (Griffith and Connor 20). Working with such students takes special teachers, special means, dedication, and determination. And yet, as Griffith and Connor demonstrate, many such students succeed only because of two-year colleges. Anne Ruggles Gere, Mike Rose, Smokey Wilson, and others have attested to the importance of community colleges in the lives of such students. Without them, millions of students would never succeed, and it is the two-year-college system within higher education that Kurt Spellmeyer has praised for proving "so successful that it now even seems prosaic"(39).

In addition to dealing with nontraditional students, two-year-college teachers have been pioneers in the teaching of writing and reading to the underprepared student. Smokey Wilson, Peter Dow Adams, John Langan, Lynn Troyka, Audrey Roth, Jane Peterson, and others are among the two-year-college teachers who have devoted their lives to finding the most effective methods of teaching basic language skills to academically unprepared students. Their knowledge exists in numerous professional articles and in textbooks they have prepared and class tested with thousands of students. Wilson has been particularly active in interrogating the nontraditional student and those needing special help with basic skills. Her scholarship, discussed in a number of published sources, is a model for others who would like to learn how to teach these students.

Most two-year-college teachers knew about diversity and multicultural students long before it became fashionable to discuss them. It may well be in the teaching of diverse students that two-year-college knowledge making will prove most valuable to future educators. ESL programs have been established in community colleges in large urban areas for many years. The teaching of reading, writing, and language skills to non-native speakers has been a priority in many two-year colleges. The two-year college has been a major factor in the assimilation of thousands of immigrants into the American mainstream. Peter Dow Adams, Mike Andalzua, Alan Meyers, and Loretta Kasper have been among those involved with knowledge making in ESL in two-year colleges. It is two-year-college teachers who most often help students navigate the border crossings necessary to move not just across poverty or social class or cultural boundaries, but also across language barriers of all kinds.

Another area in which two-year-college teachers have been knowledge makers is in the preparation of students for the world of work. This area of education is the one most alien to the academy. Many on the two-year campus have long been comfortable talking about job application letters, resume preparation, on-the-job writing, technical writing, lab reports, and other areas of applied writing because their students have been greatly concerned with such writing. Because many students enroll in one- or two-year technical programs that lead to employment after their course work, they need specialized writing courses related to their job training. This is true of nursing students, computer drafting students, office administration students, and others. English faculty often teach specialized writing courses for these students or at least assist the students with course assignments in writing centers.

Not only has the concern been with what current students might need, but two-year colleges have also often been called on to meet the needs of local businesses or industries that have a specific and immediate need for employee training. That training might be in the form of routine business letters or reports, or it might be more specialized in the form of a specific kind of technical writing. Few in university English departments routinely respond to such community needs. Yet the flexibility of most two-year-college teachers allows them to take on such teaching assignments, on campus or off.

The most hopeful areas for two-year knowledge making lie in the recent calls for new definitions of scholarship and for valuing teaching and the scholarship of teaching and learning. The plea to extend the definitions of what constitutes scholarship to include systematic inquiry through either the synthesis, interpretation, or application of knowledge as called for by the Commission on the Future of Community Colleges and the Carnegie Foundation for the Advancement of Teaching (Boyer) offers expanded opportunities to two-year-college faculty. George Vaughan has advocated valuing intellectual work other than original research, such as instructional materials, bibliographies, op-ed pieces, computer software, and technical innovations. Those represent activities with which most two-year-college teachers have had wide experience. Spellmeyer, recognizing the power of the community college, has urged a view of knowledge and knowledge making that seems compatible with the democratic spirit of two-year colleges when he suggests that "non-specialists" can be considered as knowledge makers (44).

Sidney Dobrin also has recognized the need, particularly in composition studies, to expand knowledge resources. Essential to the field's development are, he says,

> . . . multiple modes of inquiry, multiple types of knowledge. Current thinking in composition recognizes that theory and practice are not self-contained. They not only rely on each other in transformative flux but also are dependent upon continued multimodal inquiry from various locations within the field in order to continually inform rhetoric and composition. (24–25)

No one is more knowledgeable about what is needed to expand knowledge in English studies than two-year-college faculty members. They have been at the forefront of teaching writing at all levels to diverse populations. Their knowledge about literacy production and transmission is especially valuable. Their expertise in dealing with nontraditional students, with multicultural audiences, with all the attendant issues of gender, race, class, and ethnicity can be the source of valuable and useful information to all of higher education as student populations in all settings only grow more diverse and more nontraditional.

What is needed now is for local knowledge to become global and be translated into theory whenever possible. The theory must be discussed and debated. Those within two-year colleges must come to see themselves as having knowledge worth sharing with the academy as a whole. Additionally, the academy must demonstrate a willingness to consider the knowledge generated by its two-year-college counterparts. Dobrin's comments about those teaching writing are appropriate for everyone throughout higher education:

> . . . whether engaged in theoretical pursuit or consumed by teaching six sections of basic writing [compositionists] need to explore the ways in which theory from various ideological and epistemological backgrounds influences both the theoretical inquiries and the diurnal practice that makes up the field's bread and butter. (155)

## Conclusion

By virtue of their unique location, sitting as they always have *between* the university and the secondary school, two-year-college faculty are in an important position to offer knowledge about those who move on to the university and those who will move from two-year settings to the world of work. Two-year faculty themselves, occupying this interborder position are, as Howard Tinberg says, "quintessentially postmodern," possessing "no single identify, but rather have shifting and blurred identities. Like the subject of postmodern anthropology, we move in a variety of worlds. We are the educational 'mestizas,' the translatable teachers" (x–xi). Characterizing himself, he offers a profile of many two-year faculty:

> A Ph.D. steeped in literary theory and trained in the traditional canon, I strain here and in my classroom to find a language that has currency for theorists as well as for practitioners. I publish, I give papers at professional conferences, and I teach. I work to connect to all these activities; I try to translate them across borders. In my professional writing, I try to strike a balance between the public and the private, the academic and the expressive, the abstract and the classroom-based. In my teaching, I seek to use theory as guide to my practice and look to practice to engender theory. (xi)

It is this unique position that has created problems for the two-year teacher in the past, but it may well be that this position will be one of strength, a place from which the new knowledge needed by the discipline for the future can be most productively engendered.

Nellie McKay, a Modern Language Association representative to the 1987 English Coalition Conference, indicated the importance of listening to multiple professional sources of knowledge, particularly two-year-college teachers:

> . . . I was impressed by the makeup of the group and learned a great deal from listening to those who are more in the trenches than I am— not only elementary and secondary school teachers but especially from those who teach in community colleges. . . . (Elbow 1)

She goes on to suggest that those in the universities, because of the pressures for research, neglect attention to "'the teaching of reading, writing, speaking, and listening' or to the prime issues in the way students learn." It is in these essential areas that two-year-college teachers can be most helpful to their university colleagues. If two-year-college teachers will share the knowledge they have acquired from their serious attention to teaching, knowledge about transmitting ideas to varied audiences, their work with technology in varied settings, and their expertise at workforce training, they can make valuable contributions to the discipline's knowledge. They can participate in the most productive ways with their colleagues throughout the academy to educate citizens in the twenty-first century.

It is essential that higher education encourage two-year-college faculty to become more active participants in the national discussion. Two-year faculty have much to teach the discipline of English and much to contribute to the direction higher education will take in the new century. Recent trends toward valuing teaching, toward more acceptance of classroom-based research, toward more emphasis on literacy education, and toward the use of technology in classrooms highlight areas where two-year teachers possess expertise. With the recent national initiatives to assure all citizens the equivalent of the first two years of a college education, major attention is shifting to the nation's two-year colleges. As higher education becomes more expensive, society will be more inclined to support the work of two-year colleges than it will those engaged in canon debates and theory wars. If university English departments do go the way of departments of classics, as Harold Bloom has suggested (17), or dissolve into departments of cultural studies, as Michael Berube has indicated, two-year colleges will be in place and ready to assume teaching the skills of reading and writing to all of tomorrow's students.

## Works Cited

Berube, M. 1996. Address. National Council of Teachers of English Convention. Chicago Hilton, Chicago. (Nov 21.).

Bloom, H. 1994. *The Western Canon: The Books and School of the Ages.* New York: Harcourt.

Boyer, E. L. 1990. *Scholarship Reconsidered.* Princeton: Carnegie Foundation for the Advancement of Teaching.

"Casting New Light on Old Notions: A Changing Understanding of Community College Faculty." 1998. *Change* (Nov./Dec.): 43–47.

Cohen, Arthur M., and Florence B. Brawer. 2003. *The American Community College.* 4th ed. San Francisco: Jossey.

Commission on the Future of Community Colleges. 1988. *Building Communities: A Vision for a New Century.* Washington, DC: American Association of Community and Junior Colleges.

Cross, R. K. 1985. "Introduction." In *The Forge*, by T. S. Stribling. Tuscaloosa: U of Alabama P.

———. 1985. Introduction. In *The Store*, by T. S. Stribling. Tuscaloosa: U of Alabama P.

———. 1986. "Introduction." *Unfinished Cathedral*, by T. S. Stribling. Tuscaloosa: U of Alabama P.

Cross, R. K., and J. T. McMillan, eds. 1982. *Laughing Stock: The Autobiography of T. S. Stribling.* Memphis: St. Luke's.

Cowan, G., and E. Cowan. 1980. *Writing.* New York: Wiley.

Cox, K. Castellucci. 1998. "Magic and Memory in the Contemporary Story Cycle: Gloria Naylor and Louise Erdrich." *College English* 60: 150–72.

Dobrin, S. I. 1997. *Constructing Knowledges: The Politics of Theory-Building and Pedagogy in Composition.* Albany: State U of New York P.

Doucette, D., and J. E. Roueche. 1991. "Arguments with Which to Combat Elitism and Ignorance about Community Colleges." *Leadership Abstracts* 4.13. Austin: League for Innovation in the Community College.

*The ERIC Review* 1996. 5.1/2.

Gabert, G. 1991. *Community Colleges in the 1990s.* Bloomington: Phi Delta Kappa.

Gaskins, J., D. Holt, and E. Roeger. 1998. "Do Two-Year College Students Write as Well as Four-Year College Students? Classroom and Institutional Perspectives." *Teaching English in the Two-Year College* 25: 6–15.

Gere, A. R. 1996. "Stories Out of School." *Teaching English in the Two-Year College* 23: 9–18.

Griffith, M., and A. Connor. 1994. *Democracy's Open Door: The Community College in America's Future.* Portsmouth: Heinemann.

Maher, J. 1997. *Mina P. Shaughnessy: Her Life and Work.* Urbana: NCTE.

Nist, E. A., and H. H. Raines. 1995. "Two-Year Colleges: Explaining and Claiming Our Majority." In *Resituating Writing: Constructing and Administering Writing Programs,* edited by J. Janangelo and K. Hansen, 59–70. Portsmouth: Heinemann.

North, S. M. 1987. *The Making of Knowledge in Composition: Portrait of an Emerging Field.* Portsmouth: Heinemann.

Oehler, P. 1998. "A Discography of American Literature Set to Music—Part II." *Teaching English in the Two-Year College* 26: 25–28.

———. 1994. "I Sing the Body Electric: A Selected Discography of American Literature Set to Music." *Teaching English in the Two-Year College* 21: 309–16.

Pickett, N. A. 1994. "A Quarter Century and Beyond: My Story of Teaching Technical Communication." In *Two-Year College English,* edited by M. Reynolds, 134–43. Urbana: NCTE.

Pickett, N. A., A. A. Laster, and K. E. Staples. 2001. *Technical English: Writing, Reading, and Speaking.* 8th ed. New York: Addison.

Reynolds, M. 1990. "Twenty-Five Years of Two-Year College English." *Teaching English in the Two-Year College* 17: 230–35.

Reynolds, M., ed. 1994. *Two-Year College English: Essays for a New Century.* Urbana: NCTE.

Rose, M. 1989. *Lives on the Boundary: The Struggles and Achievements of America's Underprepared.* New York: Free.

Roth, A. J. 1999. *The Research Paper: Process, Form, and Content.* 8th ed. Belmont: Wadsworth.

Spellmeyer, K. 1996. "Inventing the University Student." In *Composition in the Twenty-First Century: Crisis and Change,* edited by L. Z. Bloom, D. A. Daiker, and E. M. White, 39–44. Carbondale: Southern Illinois U P.

*Teaching English in the Two-Year College.* 1996. Special Issue on Technology (October).

Tinberg, H. B. 1997. *Border Talk: Writing and Knowing in the Two-Year College.* Urbana: NCTE.

Vaughan, G. 1994. "Scholarship and Teaching: Crafting the Art." In *Two-Year College English,* edited by M. Reynolds, 212–21. Urbana: NCTE.

Wilson, S. 1997. "Acts of Defiance (and Other Mixed Messages): Taking Up Space in a Sub-Collegiate Course." *Teaching English in the Two-Year College* 24: 291–303.

———. 1994. "What Happened to Darleen? Reconstructing the Life and Schooling of an Underprepared Learner." In *Two-Year College English,* edited by M. Reynolds, 37–53. Urbana: NCTE.

# 2

## Creating Our College, Our Community, and Ourselves

### Mary Slayter

It was a particularly dismal high school faculty meeting that catapulted me into the burgeoning ranks of community college teachers in 1971. The after-school session had dragged on and on, addressing such educational concerns as whose responsibility it was to wash the dirty cups in the teachers' lounge and why some persistent ne'er-do-wells neglected to send in lists of *tardies* and *absences* every period instead of at the end of day, by which time recalcitrant students could have escaped or learned something or who knows what.

As I fled that oppressive atmosphere for the breeze of a May afternoon, I remember yelling to a colleague, "Where did you say that new community college is taking applications?" I revved the engine of my tired VW bug, spun the tires, and scattered gravel in every direction as I headed to a rented office to talk to the new college's prospective dean of instruction about an undefined job teaching yet-to-be-identified students.

Earlier, other high school teachers had cautioned me against leaving the security of a well-established system for the uncertainties of the community college, but when my despair-inspired application was accepted and I was hired, I actually came to relish the new college's lack of definition for the freedom and flexibility it provided faculty to create original structures and fresh hopes. (I remember the wicked sense of glee I felt when I announced at one of the first state-wide community college meetings I attended that our college was so new we had no policies on the subject under discussion.)

Like Lawrence Ferlinghetti's "little Charlie Chaplin man," those of us on the initial faculty of Rogue Community College (RCC) in Grants Pass, Oregon, perched uncertainly on a high wire strung between the high school and the university, teetering this way and that while many of our former colleagues predicted an early demise for this upstart educational institution. The frenzy of the first summer of the college's existence was marked by the selection of instructors whose primary common characteristic was a willingness to plunge into the unknown. And, for those like me who were completely ignorant about this level of education, it also featured a lightning tour of other community colleges in the state to see what a community college was supposed to do.

My new colleagues and I spent long days on the dandelion-infested lawns of an abandoned Job Corps site composing course outlines while the maintenance crew refurbished bunkhouses that would be converted into classrooms. Out with the urinals and bunk beds, in with the chalkboards and tablet armchairs. I can remember the initial faculty of fourteen sitting around a table in the library trying to create an organizational chart. No hierarchy would do for us; we used coins of various sizes to represent different functions on campus: a fifty-cent piece for the president; quarters, nickels, and dimes to stand for various faculty and classified positions. All the circles were then connected to form a larger circle, showing that everyone was equally important to the functioning of the school.

When the college first opened its doors in the fall of 1971, the average age of the students was 39, and the average age of the faculty was 32. Those of us who have been at the college ever since remember that heady time as the golden years, and our recollections have sustained us the way elderly couples' memories of their youthful passions rekindle their ardor and regard for each other.

In July of the summer when the college was founded, a small group of townspeople, board members, faculty, and staff gathered to dedicate the land for the campus—twenty acres leased from the federal government for a dollar a year. (The twenty acres was given to the college years later, maybe based on the premise that possession is nine-tenths of the law.) We stood around a newly raised flagpole with a donated flag while a member of the RCC Board of Education led us in the national anthem. I remember the thrill of possibilities that summer morning as I looked across the valley to Grants Pass, the small town that is the biggest in Josephine County—sky clear, flag flapping, the board chairman's voice throbbing out into the pine trees, echoing against the walls of the cafeteria.

In the days and weeks that followed, everyone displayed amazing willingness to tolerate less-than-optimal physical surroundings because of the collective resolve to create this new institution for our community. A wonderful spirit of pioneer barn raising permeated the whole venture. The Faculty Wives Association cut and sewed red curtains for all the classroom windows, coordinating their work with that of community volunteers who tie-dyed donated fabric to hang at the edge of long windows in the institutional-feeling cafeteria. The counseling and admissions staff gathered with the dean of students in his love beads and bell bottoms to paint their building a distinctive green one Saturday in early August.

Everyone employed by the college worked to make it succeed—the plant services crew trying to fill potholes in the gravel roadway between remodeled barracks buildings faster than the Oregon rains could fill them up; the switchboard operator functioning as the invisible voice of the college, welcoming and encouraging all who called; the Learning Center staff tutoring college students in calculus, physics, literature, and writing, or preparing students who hadn't graduated from high school to take GED tests; financial aid administering federally funded programs such as the Manpower Development and Training Act, work study, student need grants and loans, the GI bill, etc.; the board and administration battling to ensure that students were warm and dry and provided with restrooms and food and reference books.

The dean of instruction and the faculty established a variety of course offerings to meet the needs of prospective students, whether they intended to use RCC as a springboard to further academic training or to prepare themselves for careers in the community. (One of the strongest arguments used in promoting the college was that high school students who didn't plan to attend a four-year college needed a place to acquire postsecondary technical training.) Local advisory committees representing different trades worked with faculty and administrators to decide which vocational programs would be most useful to the region and what classes should be offered—horseshoeing, welding, automotive, heavy equipment, forestry, day care, secretarial skills, business management, food services, hospitality industries. What basic skills and knowledge should each program include in addition to hands-on work in the field? What kind of instruction would nurses, childcare providers, landscape designers, forestry technicians, and bookkeepers need for successful careers? And what classes did all these programs need from departments like ours, which provided general education? Children's literature for early childhood education students; communication skills for automotive, forestry, and other vocational classes, with the curriculum of reading, writing, speaking, and listening based on suggestions and requests from faculty, students, and employers in the different vocational areas. (At that time it was still considered respectable to have a vocation rather than a technical profession.) We offered business English, as well, but it was later taken over by the business department because the English faculty insisted there wasn't much hope of improving student writing strictly through grammar drills, and that was what the advisory committee and business faculty insisted on.

Long discussions were also held about what should be included in the two-year associate degrees for college transfer students. What would they have to read and write in preparation for future academic work and careers, and how could we find out? We asked their teachers, past and prospective; read advising guides from the Oregon State System of Higher Education; interviewed people who were employed in fields the students might enter; and read catalogs from other colleges.

We wanted to establish requirements that would provide real substance for the students' lives and that would make them capable participants in a democratic society. Our debates rested on the underlying question of what an education should provide—job skills, intellectual breadth, ability to communicate, to do more advanced academic work, to become responsible and compassionate members of society as parents, employees or employers, citizens. At every opportunity, the college president reminded us of the college's stated mission to enhance the "worth and dignity of the individual," so that we would have a community worth living in.

As I look back on it, I love the clarity of focus that drove decisions at the time—what did the students and community need, and how could we provide it? What books should be ordered for the library, and what kind of chalk and chairs for the classrooms; what should be required in each class, and how could we ensure that transfer courses truly were equivalent to offerings at four-year colleges and universities and would actually transfer? Because skeptics were offering bets that no four-year college would accept course work for credit from our little school, members of the faculty tried to sit in on comparable classes at four-year colleges and universities whenever possible to assure themselves that the instruction we offered served our students well. Visits to classes at the University of Oregon, Willamette University, Cal Tech, and Harvard, among others, reassured us that our reading lists and requirements had much in common with those more illustrious institutions, and that our students, though often lacking in formal academic background, generally approached their coursework with as much enthusiasm and dedication as their four-year-college counterparts.

As a community college faculty, we were acutely aware of the promises that had been made to local taxpayers to persuade them to vote the college into existence. Fliers urging a "yes" vote had invited the populace to approve a vocational college, a place for the seventy percent of local high school students who didn't go on to a four-year college or university, but a mark in the "yes" box ratified a legislative commitment to provide college transfer classes and adult education, as well. That hard-won affirmative vote created a comprehensive community college that required an even-handed response to a threefold charge: (1) to train workers for local business and industry, (2) to provide classes for personal enrichment and adult basic education, and (3) to offer lower-division college transfer classes needed by those with the ultimate goal of a bachelor's degree.

We plunged into our work with exuberance and conviction. Our efforts were bolstered by the unbounded confidence extended us by the administration and board, and their permission, almost a mandate, to experiment, to reach the students whatever it took. I'm sure the deans and the college president and the Board of Education had to concern themselves with the property tax revenues collected and tuition reimbursement received for full-time equivalent students (FTEs) versus money spent for salaries, equipment, and supplies, but we rarely heard about it.

Encouraged by a young dean of instruction with endless belief in our commitment and talents, we built a viable school where critics had predicted we would fail. Whenever one of us floated a bold, sometimes rash, new idea for classes past him, the dean would say, "You're the expert. Give it a try. If it doesn't work, we'll have learned something." With many of us only recently removed from public high schools where teachers were regarded as day laborers who literally needed to punch a time clock, we felt a dizzying sense of possibility coupled with an equally heavy weight of responsibility. But we determined to pull out all the stops to justify this astonishing faith in our abilities.

We tried teaching writing courses without textbooks, relying instead on current newspaper and magazine articles as texts. We asked students to keep persuasion journals ranging from editorials and advertisements to personal arguments. We sent students into the community to investigate and write about the workings of governmental, religious, and educational institutions, and we invited guest speakers to our classes who represented such disparate groups as the League of Women Voters, the John Birch Society, the Copper Canyon Press in Port Townsend, Washington, and Sandstone, a commune well-known for its experiments in open marriage. We asked students in literature classes to try their hand at writing fiction, poetry, and drama, in addition to analyzing it, and we built creative individual or group projects into the course outlines for all the introductory humanities and literature classes.

My office partner and I, both full-time, both women with small children, made up the English department. The ratio of full-time faculty to students was the best it has ever been in the history of the college. The fourteen full-time faculty members and a few part-timers handled almost all course offerings, and we had a relatively small number of students (450 FTE that first year). The ratio of women to men was another story. The only other women on the staff worked as secretaries or in the Learning Center, but I can't recall that the gender disparity was ever a subject of discussion among the faculty at large in those early years.

The college's previous incarnation as a Job Corps facility had been most famous for the claim that George Foreman learned to box during his stay there, taught by the local sheriff. The Job Corps was also notorious because it brought the first racially diverse people into a community afflicted by unconscious bigotry and unconfronted prejudice, like many rural American towns at the time.

When the college emerged from the abandoned Job Corps site, some of the long-time residents of the area—conservative, careful—transferred their misgivings about the black Job Corps students to the region's newly established commune dwellers who now mixed in equal numbers with local housewives and mill workers and small business owners who had wanted a college education for years but had been unable to leave jobs and families to attend classes forty to seventy miles away at Southern Oregon State College.

We tried to make our classes suit all of the students, but because the college had been promoted as an answer for the large number of local high school students who didn't go on to college, the vocational programs received most of the media attention: the farrier school; the automotive, heavy equipment, and welding shops; the model business office; the day care center.

I have never forgotten my one and only trip to the farrier school, a twelve-week program the president regarded highly as evidence of the college's ability to be unique. (He had horseshoe nails bent into rings, which he gave out at Chamber of Commerce and Rotary Club meetings, delighting student entrepreneurs who saw a resemblance to the spoon rings on sale at Renaissance fairs up and down the freeway most weekends.) After driving eight miles there, I encountered muscular young men learning their trade, with hammers clanging on anvils, and an ice chest full of frozen horses' hooves to practice on.

During those first years, the underlying assumption was that students came to the college because they wanted an education, and students assumed the teachers knew something about what might be important for them to master in various disciplines. It was a wonderful synchrony of students wanting to learn and teachers wanting to teach. I remember the fierce loyalty of some early students. They loved their classes, their classmates (for the most part), and their teachers.

The students came from town and country. Communes flourished at opposite ends of the county, miles into the hills, and provided a home for many disengaged, but well-educated young people intent on building a new life based on love and freedom (and, at least partially, their parents' money). Their presence had triggered a lack of neighborliness unprecedented in the area since Chinese miners came to make their fortunes during the nineteenth-century gold rush. Long-time residents were suspicious of these newcomers with long hair and flamboyant lifestyles.

Righteously indignant neighbors complained about hippies skinny-dipping in local creeks. The advent of these new settlers occasioned signs in local businesses—"Hippie patronage not solicited," and "Help wanted—No hippies need apply." The civil rights movement of the 60s had swept past this region without leaving much of a trace, but a number of students and faculty members did stage one mild sit-in at a local cafe to protest the "no-shirt, no-shoes, no-service" sign that served to bar many of our students from the premises.

It was a time when long hair and beards were certain evidence of moral decay. I remember the day we had Andrew Weil speak, the Harvard-trained M.D. who was investigating alternative medicine. He had a huge head of black hair, a bushy black beard, spotlessly clean Levi's, and a glistening white shirt with embroidered flowers rising yellow, pink, and red from its surface. To any disinterested eye, the most obvious and overpowering thing about his appearance was his cleanliness. He fairly sparkled, but I remember disgruntled writing students who had been required to attend his presentation complaining that they couldn't respond to anything that "dirty hippie" had to say. (He also horrified the audience by suggesting that marijuana might have medicinal uses, and that a certain kind of mushroom, which poked its elfin cap through the soil of most of the cow pastures in northern Oregon, was hallucinogenic.)

In the early 70s, we were still caught up in trends such as the Human Potential Movement encouraging us to "be all we could be." In addition, many of the students enjoyed the luxury of being able to take classes not just to fill requirements but simply because they wanted to add to their store of knowledge and experience. GI Bill students wanted to learn, but they also wanted to stretch out their benefits as long as they could, so they settled in quite happily to extend a two-year degree to three, four, or five. Housewives, retired military people, and senior citizens sought intellectual challenges, as did young people who had adjusted their lifestyles Thoreau-like to require very little money, and others who were subsidized by wealthy parents while they "found" themselves. Perhaps what was so exhilarating is that we were all "finding" ourselves and creating the school and the community and ourselves in the process.

Although those of us in the English department labored far into the night reading papers, studying literature, and boning up on strategies for teaching students to write memos, resumes, and work orders, we were collectively annoyed when we heard talk about the "real world" as though jobs, families, and daily existence could somehow be more "real" than reading, writing, and analyzing ideas that have perplexed and inspired humankind for thousands of years. "Do I contradict myself? Very well, then, I contradict myself. I am large. I contain multitudes." "I wished to live deliberately so when I came to die I would not find that I had not lived." "To be or not to be, that is the question." We argued that the life of the mind and spirit is at least as real as washing the dishes or mowing the lawn.

Our optimism about building a better society was undoubtedly fueled by the successes and excesses of political and social activism in the 60s and 70s. We took students to an event that Ken Kesey (author of *One Flew Over the Cuckoo's Nest* and *Sometimes a Great Notion*) organized at Oregon State University in Corvallis as part of his Bend in the River populist movement. I remember the students camped with their sleeping bags, waiting to hear Kesey, William Williams, Leo Marx, William Stafford, and Studs Terkel describe a more enlightened, more humane future.

We also attended a weeklong conference in Pasadena that was designed with the immodest but seriously held goal of making planetary life better. Buckminster Fuller, Carl Rogers, Ralph Nader, and Elizabeth Kubler-Ross were among those who agreed to participate, with concurrent conferences in Toronto and Paris all tied together by television. In order to attend, my colleagues and I traveled through the Oregon and California night in a drafty VW bus with a sliding door that wouldn't quite close, huddled under blankets and coats. As I recall, the sponsors and organizers of the conference were filled with such zeal for transforming the world that some of them mortgaged (and some of them lost) their homes to help underwrite the event.

Many of our students were idealists, too, intrigued with exploring the ultimate nature of reality. They responded eagerly to guest actors from the Oregon Shakespeare Festival who guided a room full of us, teachers, students, and administrators, through a preparation-to-acting exercise. We stood in a crooked circle in the rectangular makeshift Learning Center imagining ourselves inhaling a ball of golden light, letting it suffuse our whole being, until finally we all swore the room had become noticeably brighter.

The college administration had promised that if twelve or more people wanted a particular class, the college would try to offer it. As a result, in addition to more conventional composition and literature classes, the English faculty offered women's literature at the urging of a women's group, novel writing at the request of those who knew a successful local novelist, and an evening course in speculative literature upon the suggestion of local spiritual seekers. The latter course featured the books of Carlos Casteneda, who had studied with the mystical Yaqui healer, Don Juan. (In 1997, twenty-six years after the fact, the speculative lit teacher and I met a former student, who fondly remembered late evening get-togethers at different students' homes, and images of Tom, an apparently extraordinary class member, who was able to levitate. Cries of "He really did" echoed from teacher and student alike.)

In hindsight, some of our undertakings may appear naive or even suspect by today's more cynical standards, but we took our obligation to provide a focal point for postsecondary education in our community seriously. The humanities department met at least once a year with our counterparts at Southern Oregon State College and Grants Pass High School, and we sponsored lectures, art shows, film series, opera workshops, and poetry readings open to the community.

We created an elaborate composition program that highlighted a different discipline each month. And much to our amazement, we persuaded colleagues and administrators to block out a time in the college schedule when no other classes were offered, thus allowing everyone on campus to attend presentations required for writing classes. We organized events and chose readings with the hope that understanding and respect for people in different fields would increase relevance and coherence in the curriculum and generate additional tolerance and goodwill among colleagues, students, and community members. (The public was invited to the bimonthly presentations free of charge, and we published a collection of selected student papers each term.)

I still remember a criminal justice panel for the program, which consisted of a judge, a district attorney, a prisoner from the local jail, a police officer, and a priest. When it became obvious that the sympathies of the audience lay with the bright, likable young prisoner, the judge decided to give those in attendance the chance to commute the young man's sentence. Upon their recommendation, the judge freed the prisoner, with the admonition that the audience must take some responsibility for his future well-being. In response, students launched an extensive letter-writing campaign to provide encouragement and support.

When we realized that a large population of older citizens was being neglected, we put together an annual three-day celebration of early settlers' achievements. We arranged for rides around campus on horse-drawn wagons; fired up steam-powered tractors, balers, and logging equipment; set up demonstrations of soap making, spinning, weaving, needlework, and quilting; arranged displays of old photographs, camera equipment, and turn-of-the-century furnishings, along with collections of china, radios, crank telephones, and Victrolas.

The faculty at Rogue worked collaboratively, creating applied and interdisciplinary courses such as "Visual Images in Art and Poetry"; "Literature of Oregon" (a course that involved traveling around the state to visit writers in their own environs); an intensive, team-taught world history and world literature class; an advanced expository writing course that resulted in the publication of a book of oral histories, which students had composed after interviewing longtime residents; an interpersonal communication class scheduled on three marathon weekends for local

Probation Department volunteers; and a six-week study tour of Europe that offered credit in world literature, art appreciation, world history, and sociology.

I remember our scramble to expand academically while working in an institution where teaching was the primary focus and scholarship something to be attended to on one's own time. We bargained for a tuition waiver that would allow teachers to take classes in other disciplines without charge, and faculty members regularly took advantage of this option. My own RCC transcript shows classes in computer programming, banjo playing, Spanish, reader's theater, tennis, French, and Japanese, among others. I also participated in a teacher exchange for a term at Kapiolani Community College in Hawaii and helped lead one of RCC's first interdisciplinary trips to Europe.

Members of the humanities department formed a conference-going team, seeking sessions that would give us a larger context for studies in our disciplines. We learned about split brain research with Roger Sperry and Robert Ornstein, philosophy with James Hillman, and Sufí mysticism with Idries Shah. We heard lectures from Bruno Bettleheim, Huston Smith, David Bohm, Gregory Bateson, William Dement, and Karl Pribram. We attended writing conferences with such notables as William Stafford, Richard Hugo, Ursula LeGuin, Ken Kesey, Barry Lopez, and Diane Wakowski, and participated in yearly English conferences.

Despite our eagerness to expand our intellectual horizons, though, we resisted the impulse to take ourselves and our economic world too seriously. One of our faculty members filled out graduation application forms on behalf of Arnold, the pig that lived near a local tavern. Another slept overnight on the old sofa in our office after returning to the campus at midnight from a field trip to the Oregon Shakespeare Festival forty miles distant. Living twenty miles away and with a class at 8:00 A.M. she decided to curl up on the couch for the remainder of the night. When the business manager discovered what she had done, he sent her a bill for a night's lodging, with a warning not to use the office as a motel again. In a formal written response, she assured him she would not, complaining that the sofa was lumpy, the light irritating, and the noisy vacuums disturbing.

We had little patience for bureaucracy or pomposity. We threw the I Ching to get the basic design for our "Whither are we drifting" report, the annual departmental planning proposal. When asked to prioritize budget requests in "decision packages," we put our "decision package" list in a file folder, put the file folder in a big envelope, put the envelope in a box, and then put the box in a larger container. Wrapping it in festive-colored paper with an extravagant bow, we labeled it the Humanities Department's "decision-package package."

The first years of Rogue Community College's existence were marked by zaniness, trial and error, and nonstop work, but they also engendered a flexibility and resilience and respect for students, colleagues, and community members that have seen us through the multitude of changes and challenges since that time, and which have prepared us to cope with the demands of the Information Age in which we presently find ourselves. The reflection on how we met and solved the problems of the past should provide a foundation for the leaps into the unknown that lie before us.

# 3

## Lives Worth Fighting For

### Marilyn Smith Layton

Each year as I walk with my colleagues in graduation, following the blue gowns of our graduates, my heart and eyes always fill with awe at what the ceremony means. Looking out at the families and graduates from so many cultures and countries, I think: "This is America at its best. Here we celebrate over and over the promise of this country, reminded of that promise by those who may have even risked their lives to be here, driven by their convictions about freedom and their belief in education. In this audience each person is telling a part of the American story."

When I face a class for the first time, I imagine a large electronic globe, which marks the birth of each human life, honoring that life with a small light in a new color distinct from all other lights and lives. As people move in the world, their light tracks their movement. Each day, many lights appear; others disappear. If a class at a two-year college could be traced on that globe, the lights in it might have their origins in several decades and, frequently, in several continents. In the convergence of all these diverse lights within a classroom, I feel a sort of cosmic wonder: What will this class become for each person in it? What will its members learn? What will I learn from it?

"Genuine education begins with reciprocity between student and teacher," the poet Theodore Roethke asserts in the film *In a Dark Time*. Many years ago, those words launched me toward the insight that learning from my students was not just a good idea but essential to the process of *their* learning. The student narrator of Langston Hughes' poem "Theme for English B" also notes the reciprocal nature of learning between himself and his instructor as he struggles with the content of his required theme: "As I learn from you,/ I guess you learn from me . . ."

After more than three decades of teaching, I still marvel at the possibilities of learning in a classroom. I teach at a two-year college, I say, but the world comes to our doors. As a child, I had not been much aware of that world. My mother, not ordinarily given to passing on neat sentences of her acquired wisdom, did make one thing clear: A college degree was necessary for a woman because she needed something to fall back on in case her husband died. My mother had not gone to college, and my father was still alive and working, so I am not certain about the origins of her urgent conviction. I went, nevertheless, minus the intimation that having a degree could be anything more fulfilling than purchasing an insurance policy.

During college I had married. I graduated from Northwestern University with a B.A. in English and a baby boy whose emergence had prevented me from student teaching, earning a teaching certificate, and thus from having anything to fall back on in case my husband, who was only 25, died.

When we moved to Ann Arbor, Michigan, I was certain my life had passed me by. In an attempt to save it, I eventually spoke to an adviser at the University of Michigan who gave me a life-changing nudge: "You can spend a year here getting your teaching certificate," he said, "or you can get a master's degree in the same amount of time and with it, teach in a community college." Community college? I had never heard the words combined, but I was willing to learn and went on to complete a master's degree in English.

When my husband—still alive—and I arrived in Seattle in 1968 for his continuing studies at the University of Washington, I discovered that North Seattle Community College was being built. Eventually I met with the English chair at Seattle Central Community College, and three days before classes were to begin in September 1969, I received a call from him.

"I'd like you to teach two classes of composition—English 101," he intoned, "one on Monday evening, and one on Tuesday evening. At Nathan Hale High School, for North Seattle Community College." I checked with my (former) husband, who told me I could only be gone one night a week. Astonishingly, I complied.

I had three days to prepare to teach my first class and to create a syllabus for the quarter. I had a master's degree in English, but no grounding whatsoever in the art and pedagogy of composition. I called an English-teacher friend who provided me her copy of Sheridan Baker's *The Practical Stylist*. When Monday night came, I decided against trying to teach information only forty-eight hours old in my brain and went to class instead with some poetry of John Donne.

I taught one of my favorite poems that first night, and then called upon a man from Holland, an engineer from Boeing who had returned to brush up his writing skills. "Why are you teaching poetry in this composition class?" he asked.

My heart beating visibly beneath a heavy, prim wool dress, I responded by proceeding with my lesson plans: "We are going to use this poem tonight to write about love," I said. "Please take out some paper and write."

I remember that engineer and that class like a mother in love with her first-born. He said something else to me that quarter that stuck: "You have a good education and you are a good teacher. You know much from books. But you know nothing about the lives your students live—lives like Gerald's in our class, a man who drives a mail truck."

His comment humbled me at the same time that it opened for me the desire and the challenge to learn from my students as much as I could about their lives, perceptions, and dreams. That was my first lesson in the truth I later encountered in the words of Roethke.

I taught one class each week all that first year. One comment from a student evaluation that year was particularly compelling and insightful: "You seem uncomfortable with your own authority," she said. She was right. One grows into a sense of authority slowly sometimes, especially when not conditioned as a child to exercise it.

When North Seattle Community College officially opened its doors in 1970, an unpretentious president from Kansas was there to welcome a new faculty assembled from the old ranks of its sister college, Seattle Central, along with a few lucky folks on contract and a bunch of part-timers—I among them—who were soon to discover their exploited status. For over five years, I taught as a part-timer; in January 1975, I received a full-time position and contract, and the following September, tenure at the college.

The students who filed through our open doors in those early years were familiar to the faculty, had English as their first, and usually, only language, and differed most from their instructors in having to juggle both work and student life rather than returning to dormitories and meals waiting for them, privileges many of us had known, with our afternoons and evenings free to study and to sleep.

I taught in those early years mostly as I'd been taught, but the clouds of anxiety under which the concrete fortress of the college had been erected in the late 1960s—the national despair over our country's certain march toward death in Vietnam, both for the Vietnamese and our own young people—eventually found their way onto our quiet campus. As a faculty, we were beginning to doubt ourselves in the classroom.

As the decade of the 1970s unfolded, a strange phenomenon became obvious in the halls of the college. Languages other than English floated through the air, and new faces, many from Southeast Asia, began to enter our classes. These students did not share our pasts, and we could no longer assume what they needed to learn.

In the fall of 1979, a sad but articulate young man named Tang introduced me to what I had only read about in the news. He wrote about his
journey on the enormous surface of the ocean in a small fishing boat
floating to an aimless point, with twelve exhausted people trying hard to
save their leaking boat from sinking. Tang remembered his mother's
words as he lay in his boat, too weak to stand up. She had told him that
if he chose to make this journey, he must accept the real possibility of
death. Should he succeed, her wish for him was to study and work. Of
his first moments in the United States nearly two years later, Tang wrote
of himself in the third person, a young boy lost in a completely unknown
world where dogs wore coats and women painted their eyes—a world
he had nearly lost his life to reach.

Another student from Vietnam, Paul, concluded one of his essays by
stating that he had not come to this country to pursue luxury and fantasy
but for the attraction of liberty and the freedom of choice. He believed
in this country as a place that could give him the chance to work on whatever he chose with lots of promise and encouragement.

If English instructors are burdened by the weight of reading papers,
they are also enriched by the vistas those papers provide. My long experience as a teacher has convinced me of the rich intelligence and experience that people carry within them, so often unexpressed and thus
unaffirmed, indeed, so often unrealized by even themselves. People must
be valued by others in order to learn to value themselves. I've said about
myself that the times I most need love, I am the least lovable. Too many
children grow up longing to be recognized, to be loved. The two greatest needs a human being has, a counselor advised a faculty development
institute in Seattle a few years ago, are, first, to belong, and second, to
be competent.

When we neglect to value and affirm a person's life, that person will
often make others pay. The filmmaker Hal Hartley captures these dynamics succinctly in his analysis of incompetence:

> I have found that all incompetence comes from not paying attention,
> which comes from people doing something that they don't want to do.
> And doing what you don't want to do means either you have no choice,
> or you don't think the moments of your life are worth fighting for.
> (quoted in de Jonge 21)

Many people do not perceive the possibility of choice in their lives;
others lack the conviction that their lives are, indeed, worth fighting
for, especially if no one has helped them to believe in their own worth.
In a speech I heard writer Alice Walker give, she made this assertion:
"Everyone's life must be paid for by someone else." And then she
asked, "Who has paid for you, for your life?" Initially, I responded to

her question on a literal level, remembering that when I went to college, my father's name appeared on the line that asked, "To whom should the tuition bill be sent?" Of course as I have grown older, I understand more every day what it means to pay for another human being's life—the constancy of being present for that person, of making my contributions, if such they are, appear effortless and without price. Over the years, I have learned again and again that it is not easy, though it is essential, to use my life as a teacher so that others may flourish without being in my debt.

Today, fewer and fewer young people have the luxury of naiveté about these matters. They cannot depend on the support and availability of parents, family, teachers, and community—cannot make it even into their teens without keen awareness that their caretakers have other demands on their lives, sometimes obviously more pressing than the child's.

Some students have a sense of neglect written in their cells—the way they have learned to slump in a constricting tab-chair, the way they stop seeing even with their eyes open—the certain knowledge they radiate that their lives are not worth fighting for. Tom was such a student. Responding to an assigned essay that had asked students to document a life-changing lesson they had learned, his essay began with a declaration that when you grow up in the city, life seems insignificant. People don't respect you or each other. As a kid in the city, he learned not to respect people or even other people's right to live. He wrote about playing with toy guns as a child and wanting to experience the power of knowing he could kill, about growing up around violence and death, about having guns pulled on him, and about an aunt stabbed to death, about being unable to cry at her funeral. He claimed to have no emotions toward the loss of human life.

The pivotal night for Tom's reconsidering the meaning of death came unexpectedly for him when, returning across town with a friend, he stopped to witness a brawl between two men outside a tavern. Suddenly, one man shot the other. Tom stood there across the street, staring at the pool of blood now forming on the wet pavement, watching the man who had been shot cover the bullet hole with his hand, let out his last breath, and close his eyes. His paper concluded with Tom's realizing for the first time that when people get shot they don't get up and play again. From this moment, he gained respect for life, both other people's and his own. The week after he saw the man get shot, he cried for the first time over his aunt. I cried, too, reading his paper, for the young boy who had only gained respect for life by seeing a human being die.

When Casey appeared in my first-quarter composition class, her clear and attentive eyes and smile carried only questions: Was she going to be disappointed in this class? Was I going to make it worth her while? She wrote her first few papers competently but without conviction—without a sense of her own voice. About halfway through the class, she discovered it when asked to write about food. Her mother had first eaten pizza as a young girl in Chicago and had once dreamed of opening a pizza parlor in the West. Although the essay developed the subsequent rituals of making and eating pizza in their home, I wanted to know more about where Casey's mother had first eaten pizza in Chicago in those early days of its emerging popularity.

"Ask your mother more about it," I suggested, when Casey came by my office to talk about revising her draft. "I can't," she said.

"Why not?" my eyes must have asked.

"She died last year," Casey said, a few seconds later.

When I could speak again, we talked more about Casey's life. She had grown up in White Center, near Seattle, had lost her father when she was twelve, her mother eight years after that. She had come to college on her own a year later at twenty-one, the first in her family to attend college. Her sophisticated command of English came from her love of reading, but she was forging her own way in a family who had big doubts about indulging in the frills of higher education.

When I had Casey in another class the following spring in a course called "Rituals Across Cultures," she wrote an autobiographical essay on grieving:

> The worst thing about American grieving is that the very essence of it—the choking and stifling of pain—leaves the true object of grief—healing and the acceptance of loss—unfinished. This is why the loss of my mom brought with it all of the past pain of losing my dad. I had never in a true sense grieved the loss of him.
>
> Now I remember clearly watching my dad's thick wavy hair fall away from his scalp with chemotherapy. I remember seeing his face grow gaunt, and his Italian skin grow pale. I remember spending long afternoons at Highline Hospital with him, while he joked with the nurse—brown eyes flashing. Eventually even his noisy eyes grew quiet and dim with illness. In our home, in a rented hospital bed, he slipped into a coma. It was there, in his room, where I saw him last. I was unable to comprehend our parting. I went back to school two days after his death. I made the honor roll that year, but forgot him—and cheated myself of much needed healing. Now I don't fight these memories, but welcome them. They are like the itching of a cut that is repairing itself; they are the hallmarks of healing [. . .].
>
> Life is good—but for now the loss of my parents is my autobiography. Someday, my loss will only be a fraction of me, and I look forward to the day when the phrase 'My parents are dead' will not define me."

How could I have known, looking through those clear light brown eyes, that so much sadness had already underpinned Casey's strength?

At a conference several years ago, I met an instructor from Duke University. In a conversation about the challenges of teaching, he said that when in rare cases he was able to motivate his students to see past their BMWs and designer jeans, he could sometimes imbue them with the excitement of learning.

"The BMWs and the designer jeans are not my problems as a teacher," I said, smiling. "I have to motivate students to see past their failures, beyond their idea of themselves as incompetent learners. When *that* happens, the rest can happen."

In another composition course in the mid-1980s, a student named Kevin arrived in class the first day and every day thereafter spankingly dressed in a dark suit and tie. The first day of class, he asked students to line up their chairs more neatly. Soon he became a willing object of humor. He was not from a military background as some students suspected, but a businessman who had made money by inventing and selling grease-removing exhaust systems to restaurants.

His first essay, entitled "I'm Not Sorry," began with this paragraph:

> The most important knowledge a child receives is at home with the parents. Home is where love and support can strengthen, where neglect and disapproval destroys. Home is truth where self-esteem is molded. This is where I first learned from my parents that I was different from all the other children. I was a slow learner, I was dumb, stupid. I was simply a problem to everyone I was around.

I asked Kevin at the time for a copy of that essay, but he never provided it for me.

As the term progressed, so did Kevin, but although he had learned to work hard, he could not overcome all his previous academic struggles in one quarter's course in English. The grade of *B* that I gave him at the end of that class was tenuous in my mind—a tribute to effort, emerging ability, and consistent work. I thought he would be pleased with it. He wasn't.

He turned our school upside down in his effort to have the grade changed to an *A*. He contacted my administrator, my intern from that quarter, and every student who had been in the class. He came by to see me and to argue, semipleasantly, about it. I provided him with every bit of documentation that I had, but I feared his anger. He told me that this obsession for an *A* had even ruined his honeymoon, because he could talk of nothing else.

I held firm. So did he. One day, perhaps eight months into this battle of wills, just as I had finished teaching my morning classes and the students from the last class had all left, the door of the classroom opened and there, filling its frame, stood Kevin.

I suspected my life was close to its end.

"Just wanted to come by and let you know I finally understand your grade," he said smiling. "Sorry for all the problems I've caused."

"What gave you this new understanding?" I said, wanting to sound casual before I fainted.

"It just came to me. That's all.

A week later, when I was again alone at the end of the morning, Kevin reappeared. I thought maybe he had reverted to his angst.

"Remember how you always stressed the value of being able to communicate?" he said. "Remember how you praised a liberal education?"

I guessed I remembered, but I wanted to know why Kevin was remembering.

"When I get my associate of arts degree, I want to go to your university, Northwestern. I want to know if you'd be willing to write a letter of recommendation for me."

I, write a letter of recommendation for this man? "Kevin," I said, " you made life hell for me for many months, fighting a just grade." I needed time to think about his crazy request. "Come back in a few days."

When he returned, I told him I would write the letter, but that I would have to include some mention of his unforgettable fight with me and the college over his grade. He smiled, said he understood, thanked me, and left.

After writing that letter, I called Kevin to read it to him so that he might reject it in favor of some other source of support.

"Send it on," he said. "Thank you."

I did not hear from Kevin for a few months after that conversation. One June day, he stopped by my office with a dozen white roses and news of his acceptance to Northwestern. He also had a person he wanted me to meet: his five-month old son, Kevin, Junior. "I want him to be in your class eighteen years from now, so don't retire until he is."

That is the first part of the Kevin story. The next year happened to be my twenty-fifth anniversary of graduating from Northwestern, and uncharacteristically, I went to celebrate. Before I left home, I called Kevin, from whom I had not heard, to see if he'd like to meet me during cocktails. He arrived on time, but his news was not good: He was on academic probation. An old college friend of mine had a son, Andy, in one of Kevin's classes who had, without knowing the connections, told his mother of this strange older guy in his class.

Perhaps it was my own disappointment for Kevin that made me forget the camera I'd brought along to take his picture, but at the airport the next day, I called him to ask if he'd take a picture of himself on the campus, maybe one with Andy for the pleasure of the coincidence.

He said he would.

I didn't hear from Kevin the following year, when he might have graduated. One day, in November, a brown envelope was waiting for me, sealed, in my college mailbox. Inside were a letter, a photograph, and a copy of the first essay he'd written in English composition, the first paragraph of which I've quoted. And here's the letter, in full:

> Dear English 101 Teacher,
> Where have I been?
> Do you remember when you told me that you wanted a copy of this [enclosed essay]? I wasn't ready to give it up. Now I have children and can. Do you remember when you gave me an assignment? "Take a picture" in Evanston. It took a few years to get it to you. Assign completed. Yes I did graduate. Do you remember me telling you I was on probation? From probation to Dean's List. Final quarter was strait [sic] A (one was an A–). I will be in touch real soon.
> Sincerely,
> Kevin

Kevin's triumphant story, nevertheless, underscores a dark and often unacknowledged element of the classroom: a teacher's vulnerability. As public figures, we can become unwittingly immersed in the private torments of those who enter our classes. Having had thousands of students in my classes over the years, I have occasionally worried about the dangers of a person's ominous lack of self-control. The conflicts of learning—coupled with broken cars, empty wallets, and sickness—sometimes push people beyond self-control. No amount of experience or anticipation could have prepared me for Kevin's response to his grade of *B*.

I think the nature of public service includes such vulnerability, but its rewards more than compensate. Albert Schweitzer said, "I don't know what your destiny will be, but one thing I know: the only ones among you who will be really happy are those who have sought and found how to serve." Certainly, I have found Schweitzer's promise a far greater portion of my work.

My years of two-year-college teaching have been shaped by enormous changes. What I learned as an undergraduate and graduate student has not turned out to be what I've needed to know and to teach. I had little insight about the nature of the process when I began teaching. I had studied literature; I began by teaching composition. I had studied only the writers of Britain and a few early writers from the United States; I teach the literature of writers from all over the world, mostly contemporary. I had once hoped that I could somehow finish my years as a teacher without having to incorporate the use of those ubiquitous computers fully into my teaching, but, of course, such thinking only reflected the fears that this old dog had about being able to learn new tricks, and thus landed me precisely and appropriately in the same mental space of fear that so many students occupy as they enter our classrooms.

I did not welcome these changes, but each has helped me to live more comfortably in a confusing and fluctuating world. What has not changed over my decades of teaching and learning is my conviction about the vitality of the two-year college as one of the premier institutions of democracy in the United States even though its bounties, as we know, are too often appreciated primarily by those who teach and learn there. When Paul referred in his essay to the country that could give one the chance to work on whatever he wanted to become, he was, unknowingly, describing not only the United States but also the country of the two-year college.

Deborah, who had come to North Seattle Community College in her late twenties, narrated her discoveries—and typical public misconceptions—at a fund-raising event: "When I'm asked what I do by someone I've just met or haven't seen in a while and I say I'm in college, their eyebrows and the pitch of their voice rise in approval. Without fail, the next question is 'Where?'" When she answers, "their eyebrows drop with a thud, and I get that sideways glance followed by a falsely lilting 'Oh.' I can only assume that the lack of enthusiasm I've encountered towards the community college can be attributed to the cause of most inaccurate impressions: ignorance."

Deborah's father was a survivor from Hungary of the Nazi Holocaust; when she was fifteen, the "long reaching effects of the concentration camp took [her] father's life. When Papa died," she explained, "his dream of an education for me died too. I couldn't go to college if he wouldn't be there to see me graduate. I couldn't marry without Papa to walk me down the aisle. Back then, I couldn't even walk past his chair in the living room. So, after high school I spent ten years doing anything that had nothing to do with my father."

During those ten years, Deborah worked as a nanny, an actress in Los Angeles, a flipper of hamburgers at a fast-food joint, and eventually, a manager at a fancy steak house with the perk of driving a company car. "It became obvious," she noted, "that selling steaks and driving a car with the words 'Prime Beef' emblazoned on the side in red letters was the best 'career' I could hope for—and the most unfulfilling thing I had ever done." She finally knew she belonged in school, but like so many students, had no idea where to start.

She describes the discoveries that followed her enrollment at a two-year college: "What I found were people not only my age, but every age. People who were there as I was, because something or someone had blown them off course and they had somehow made it back, or had been blown *on* course by some unique series of events. In our vastly different stories, backgrounds, and heritage, we are, in a sense, the same, having come to the same place [. . .]. We are becoming equipped here to change the world, not merely to function within it. At least we're acquiring the confidence and knowledge to try."

Deborah stopped for a breath at that point, but her audience needed time to breathe as well. "College resurrected desires and expectations for my life that I thought had died forever with my father. The desire to become. And the desire to help others become." Describing finally her plans to become an English teacher and to pursue her bachelor's degree in education, she had one last observation: "My mentors here have shown me that a good teacher always remains a student, never forgetting that in every seat, every term, sits someone that can teach something, and someone that can learn something."

The shelves of my literary heritage are lined not only with books from my own reading and education, but also with the stories and papers of many of the thousands of two-year-college students I have been privileged to learn from and to teach. They continue to inspire me and to remind me, again and again, of the resilience of the human spirit and the power of its will.

## Works Cited

de Jonge, P. 1996. "The Jean-huc Godard of Long Island." *The New York Times Magazine* 4 (Aug.): 21.

*In a Dark Time*. 1964. Produced by David Myer. San Francisco State College Poetry Center. Contemporary films.

# 4

## The Lesson Plan

### Richard Williamson

## Introduction

From the beginning, the community college has been a weed in the garden of academe, popping up everywhere, ragged and resilient. Over time it sprouted variously as a trade school, as an ennobling "people's college," and as a last resort for potentially lost generations. Sometimes it has flowered as all of these at once. If the two-year college were a person, we would say that it has grown up with an identity problem.

Not surprisingly, it has matured into an institution with incurable multiple personalities, though because of that, it isn't an "institution" in the usual sense. It's hard to imagine an academy that denies admission to no one and promises all who enter that they will overcome any educational deficiencies and emerge as firefighters or chefs, cinematographers or astronomers. Perhaps because it's so unlikely, the community college has turned out to be the "institution" ideally suited to serve a postindustrial populace chronically afflicted with feelings of powerlessness, bewilderment, and displacement.

At first, and even now, I suspect, no one was given specific directions on how to teach in such an eclectic place. In lieu of training for two-year-college teachers, there was only the classic Zen question: "If you do not get it from yourself, where will you go for it?" Consequently, the community college as we know it was in large part wrought by those who taught there, as they taught there.

## The Journey

The notice nailed to the door of St. John's Armenian Orthodox Church one April morning in 1952 lacked the fire and eloquence of Luther's 95 Theses, perhaps, but its effect on those of us majoring in journalism was just as profound: "JOUR 152 cancelled," it said. "Check with Registrar."

By 1952, San Francisco State College (later University) had outgrown its Victorian-era Buchanan Street campus, and classes were scattered among neighborhood parish halls and meeting rooms. For us, St. John's was "Hearst Hall," because all journalism classes were scheduled there.

The woman behind the counter in the registrar's office seemed obtuse and uncooperative when I asked her about the class. "But when will it be reinstated?" I said.

She turned back to her papers. "Never."

"But I'm a third-year journalism major. I need that class."

She looked up and smiled indulgently. "Mm-hmmmm. There is no journalism major. The Levering Act, you know. Maybe you'd better talk to the dean of language arts."

One of the saddest manifestations of the national paranoia generated during the Korean War was passage of the Levering Act establishing a loyalty oath for public employees. Included in the law was a list of organizations deemed by the U.S. Attorney General as "subversive" or, worse, "communist." Though named for its author, there was bitter poetry in the title of the Levering Act, for its purpose was levering out of public service those persons considered by some others as "undesirable."

Later it was said that of the five members of the San Francisco State journalism faculty, three could not sign the oath because of past membership in organizations on the Attorney General's list; the other two resigned in sympathy and protest.

The head of language arts seemed as perplexed as I was by the evaporation of journalism. She squeaked back in her chair, distancing herself from my complicity in the problem, and explained that it seemed unrealistic for me to start a language arts major this late in my education.

"But maybe there's something we can do," she said. She leaned forward again, folding her hands on the desk. She proposed that I enroll in some traditional language arts courses during my final year. "Maybe Psychology through Literature," she said, "and a course in the sonnets, or some poetry classes. When you complete them, we'll grant you a special degree. It will be a contract B.A., crafted especially for you."

And so it came to pass. A year later, I was awarded a bachelor of arts degree in "Language Arts with a Mass Media Emphasis."

Within three weeks of commencement, my student deferment had expired, and I was inducted into active duty in the Naval Reserve. It's been more than forty years since I stood before the officer assigning me to a duty station, but I have no trouble recalling the pink planet of his head or the half-chewed cigar blooming in the corner of his mouth.

He had much to say about college boys like me, but in the end he assigned me to an admiral's staff to work with the education officer helping other enlisted men acquire high school diplomas. As I saluted and turned to leave, he said, "Oh, and one more thing, sailor. It says here that you're a mass media expert." He curled the words derisively. "Well, then, we're gonna give ya some training in film." It may be trite, but it's definitely not wrong to say that when he raised his arm to dismiss me with a salute, he had a hand in my future.

By the time I was discharged from the Navy, San Francisco State had moved onto its new Lake Merced campus, and the language arts division had a building of its own. There were new desks, new chalkboards, and lots of new ditto machines; but the comforting odor of Lysol and old pages that always identifies a school already permeated the corridors, as though tradition had been crated and moved across town. Journalism had been restored as a major, but I'd lost interest in it. I enrolled then at State as a candidate for a master of arts degree in language arts, this time with no "emphasis." Oddly, I no longer remember what career I thought I might derive from such a program. In the broad light of retrospection, though, it's clearly a program that couldn't have been less practical.

One semester I read *Beowulf*; in the next, I took a course in Middle English. In a Shakespeare class, rather than merely reading the tragedies for explication, we performed them. I studied linguistics and completed Advanced Studies in the Principles of Modern Grammar. I followed with the Development of English Prose and then came to know the Romantics intimately.

By this time, S.I. Hayakawa, who had joined the faculty before I'd been inducted into the Navy, was known as one of the university's leading scholars. I enrolled in his Semantics and Communication Theory course and immediately became a convert to the doctrine of general semantics. By thus joining the choir of acolytes attending him, I was appointed as his reader and a section lecturer for the next two years.

Shortly after returning to school, I had been summoned to the office of my graduate advisor to discuss my thesis. The room smelled of Naugahyde, and the midday sunlight punching through the window made my eyes water. My advisor sat at his desk in silhouette.

"So, Williamson, what do you propose as a thesis topic?"

"Well, uhm, I thought I'd like to do something on Steinbeck."

The truth is I had no thesis to propose.

"C'mon, Williamson," the silhouette had said. "The library's full of papers on Steinbeck, and they only contradict each other." Then, with the passion of an evangelist, he proposed a statistical study. "Quantitative, Williamson, that's the kind of work we need now. Quantitative!" Ultimately, the topic we decided on was "Three National Stereotypes from *Life* and *The Reader's Digest*, 1935–1950."

For the next two years I spent tedious weekend hours leafing through hundreds of issues of *Life* and *The Reader's Digest*. At every reference to a German, a Japanese, or a Russian, I would slip each noun, verb, adjective, or adverb, as well as the qualities of every photograph, into one or another of dozens of categories in a complicated "instrument" that I'd had to devise beforehand. The results, of course, were so predictable the study needn't have been done in the first place: As World War II raged and subsided and the Cold War expanded, we spoke of these nationalities differently. Good guys became bad guys and vice versa. No one, I'm sure, has ever read the finished study. As for finding a vocation based on such unfocused graduate studies, just when I might have despaired, I was offered a teaching position.

In 1956, with two vicious jolts, an earthquake had almost brought down the Lake Merced campus even before it was fully constructed. Floors in the library split open, and the building had to be closed. The glass-walled student union fell in shards and two years later still hadn't been rebuilt. Scattered in its place, a few Quonset huts served as a student center. One May afternoon in 1958, I sat on a sofa in one of the huts with the person I had seen as the mysterious man in the brown suit.

He'd been on campus every day for a week before I met him. I'd seen him close in conversation with various professors, and once he sat behind the counter in the language arts office culling folders from a file. Observed through the paranoia of the time, he appeared conspiratorial and as furtive as an agent of the FBI. Then one day my advisor stopped me in the hall. "Ah, Williamson. Listen, come by my office at 4:00 this afternoon. There's someone I want you to meet."

He was introduced as Dr. Joseph Cosand, president of Santa Barbara Junior College, but as I shook his hand, he winked and said, "Call me Joe." When the advisor offered to leave the office so that we could talk undisturbed, he said, "No, no, no, you stay here! I'm going to take, um . . . say, do you mind if I call you Richard? I'm going to take Richard to the student union for coffee."

Mannerisms that had appeared sinister when I had watched Joe Cosand from a distance became paternal and caring in the coffee hut. He leaned in as he spoke, looking directly into my eyes, as though reading my responses on a screen. He explained that what was called Santa Barbara Junior College had for years been nothing but a trick of administrative sleight-of-hand. The deception was simple: The school board had gathered together all of their existing adult education courses, which were financed by those enrolled in them, and called them a college. But by establishing this illusory college, they were then able to increase property taxes, which they used solely for more generous funding of the high school. When this fiscal legerdemain had been exposed, the "college" lost accreditation.

"Now they want a real college, and they think I'm going to give them one." He bellowed a laugh. "And that's exactly what I'm going to do."

As though reciting a canon, he described in detail a college with the three-tiered curriculum familiar to us today: transfer, vocational, and remedial programs. Where classes formerly had been held at night in the high school, he said, he had acquired an ideal campus, the abandoned building of Santa Barbara State College, abolished when the University of California opened in nearby Goleta. Enthusiasm is infectious, and for a moment as he told me his plans, I glimpsed Utopia, spectral in the smoky din of the coffee hut. Its portals were doorless, inviting all to enter.

"And that's what I want to talk to you about." He told me that he was looking for someone to develop the English curriculum for non-transfer students, though he used the ghoulish label current at the time, "terminal-track students." "Like welders and secretaries," he said. When I replied that I didn't think I was a teacher, he reminded me that I had taught in the Navy and that I was now teaching a class in semantics.

"Well, maybe I teach, but I'm not an English teacher."

He looked down and didn't speak for a long moment. With his fingers he nipped pieces from his disposable foam cup, scalloping the rim. Finally he said, "If they're given traditional English instruction, I know these students will lose interest and drop out of school. What I see for them is a program developed around the critical study of mass communications. Movies, magazines, things that already interest them."

Then, meticulously, he began to fit the wedges of disposable foam back in the rim of the cup. "Now that's where you come in. First, you've had three years of journalism, isn't that so? Second, you have a degree in mass media. You had film training in the Navy, and though I haven't read it yet, your thesis analyzes popular periodicals. Am I right? Besides that, you have a solid foundation in linguistics and semantics."

He leaned forward and stood the reconstructed cup on the table before us, then smiled for the first time in many minutes. "Well, then! I'd say you're exactly the teacher I'm looking for, wouldn't you?"

In the weeks following my acceptance of Cosand's offer, always amenable to fancy, I developed a new image of myself. I began to see in my mirror another Hayakawa, a charismatic scholar distributing intellectual largess amongst faithful followers. In the words of T.S. Eliot, though, "Between the idea/ And the reality/ [. . .] Falls the Shadow."

Once I arrived in Santa Barbara, the reality was that I would work in the classroom twenty hours a week. I was given only one section of the nontransfer course I had been hired to devise, and it met daily at seven in the morning. In addition I was given two sections of freshman composition for transfer students. Two nights a week, until ten o'clock, I was to teach an adult education Shakespeare class. Most worrisome, though, I was put in charge of the remedial reading program. "Sufficient unto the day," Matthew had warned, "is the evil thereof."

## The Destination

Mercifully, the solvents of time and age have effaced my memories of that dark period, except for some scraps around the edges. I can remember, for instance, feeling as spent as a long-distance runner from racing nightly through textbooks just to stay a few pages ahead of my classes. I remember in the reading course relying on a homely wooden device that I had found in a storeroom among broken typewriters and mutilated textbooks. A handyman's whimsy, constructed in someone's garage, it was a makeshift tachistoscope for increasing a user's speed in recognizing words and phrases. I called it the "guillotine," for with the trip of a lever, a wooden blade chopped down flashing the words to be perceived.

However, if I was tentative and graceless as a reading teacher, I thought, surely I knew how to conduct a class in Shakespeare. After all, I had just completed a graduate course in the tragedies.

"Shakespeare didn't write literature," I said to open the first class. I waited a moment to give such heady stuff time to steep. "He was an actor, and he wrote scripts for actors to perform on the stage. He never intended his plays to be read and analyzed in a classroom such as this." I paused again and looked around the room to see if anyone was taking notes. "So: we're going to do something different, something Shakespeare himself would do. I'm going to assign each of you a part in *Richard the Third*, and. . . ." If I remember correctly, I never even finished my proposal.

Because it was an adult education class, the students were mostly middle-aged and had enrolled in just the one course. They weren't in class to play, they told me. They were paying for someone, and speaking pointedly they said "an authority on Shakespeare," to tell them what the lines meant and what the plays were about. I can't recall the rest of the semester now, but no doubt that's what I did, using the notes at the bottoms of the pages.

Forever in my consciousness, though, embedded like shrapnel, will be the recollection of how I taught, or to be honest, didn't teach, composition. "Maybe I teach, Joe," I had said, "but I'm not an English teacher." There was only one available solution to this problem: In both style and substance, each of my classes became a re-creation of my own graduate courses.

When I should have explained subject and verb agreement, I talked about the differences in synthetic and analytic languages. Where discussion of structure and cohesiveness would have been helpful, I described how Benjamin Lee Whorf had taken apart the language of the Hopis and then put together his theories of "anthropological linguistics." In response to simple questions about grammar and usage, I recited long passages of the *Ancren Riwle* as illustration.

Many years later I was to tell groups of student teachers for whom I was mentor and supervisor, "There's one thing to remember. When you're not having a good time teaching, then it's time to get out, because you're not going to be any good at it, anyway. And you only have fun in the classroom when you're learning. If you're not learning, you're already embalmed." It was, I believe, in the spring of 1961 that I acknowledged this truth for myself. But I hadn't reckoned with what Giuseppe Verdi celebrated as "the force of destiny."

Earlier that spring, several weeks into the semester, a young woman had come to me and pleaded for admission to my nine o'clock comp class. She was transferring, she said, from St. John's College in Maryland. She portrayed herself as a refugee from what she characterized as the tyranny of the St. John's "great books" curriculum. At first I tried to dissuade her, but she so deftly deflected each of my objections that I finally agreed to add her to the roll.

Then, about halfway through the semester, on a morning hot and gauzy with humidity, I was walking to my office after the nine o'clock class when the young woman caught up with me and suggested we walk a ways together.

"So, Miss Hutchins," I said. We still addressed students formally in those days. "I hope the lecture wasn't too academic this morning. Count Korzybski and his axioms can be pretty daunting. 'The map is not the territory, the word is not the thing,' for example." I laughed. "Just think of it as something like 'Sticks and stones may break my bones, but names will never hurt me,'" and she laughed with me.

We stepped for a moment into the latticework of light and shade beneath a pepper tree. What she really wanted to talk about, she said, was her father. She told me he was a teacher and that he wanted to meet me. Santa Barbara was still small enough then that all of us who taught—at the university, at the college, and in the high school—knew each other, at least by name.

"Your father's a teacher? What's his name?"

"Robert," she said. "Have you heard of him?"

I think everyone associated with higher education in the 1960s had heard of Robert Maynard Hutchins. He was seen as an educational radical by some and a traditionalist by others, but everyone agreed he was a prodigy. When he was only thirty, he became president of the University of Chicago, and from that position he began to challenge educational policies that had long been considered indisputable.

If he was a radical, it was in the original sense of the word, some-one who gets at the root of things. As a prodigy himself, he lamented the entrapment of precocious children in a system that moved them, as though up a broad staircase, hand in hand, from the fourth grade to the fifth, from the fifth to the sixth, and so on. While he was at Chicago, he initiated more flexible placement, allowing, for example, a twelve-year-old boy of mathematical genius to be admitted to an upper-division physics course while he was still enrolled in middle-school English and history classes. Hutchins' distrust of using age to determine someone's learning ability later led to his vigorous advocacy of continuing educa-tion for all adults.

But prodigies can be quirky. Though incurable as an innovator, Hutchins was also chairman of the board of editors for the *Encyclopae-dia Britannica*, an associate director of the Ford Foundation, and presi-dent of the Fund for the Republic, appointments that certainly qualified him as a traditionalist. At about the time that I had accepted my position on the junior college faculty, Hutchins had moved to Santa Barbara to establish and direct the Center for the Study of Democratic Institutions. Perhaps most significant, though, he was the architect, along with Mor-timer Adler, of the "great books" program, in which all learning derives from close study of history's 100 greatest books.

We had moved from the shade back into the acid sunlight.

"Wait a minute. Your father is Robert Hutchins? Robert Maynard Hutchins? Uhhh, I don't understand. Didn't you just . . . ?"

She wrinkled her nose and grinned, then told me I was invited to their house on Sunday because they were going to make ice cream.

Hutchins came through the French doors onto the terrace carrying a bowl of strawberries. He seemed extraordinarily tall to me, not just phys-ically, but in the way that saints and holy men are depicted in primitive paintings, bigger than everyone else, signifying their divinity. He smiled broadly. "Sorry I wasn't here when you arrived. When I'm writing, I lose my sense of time. Have the kids been taking good care of you?"

For maybe an hour, three of us—his daughter, her fiancé, who had also abandoned St. John's to come west with her, and I—had taken turns at the churn of an old wooden ice cream maker. Finally the girl had called to her father that we were now ready for the strawberries.

"Yes, sir. They've been giving me music lessons." I cocked my thumb at a portable phonograph from which dark and feral tones suf-fused the air. "Miriam Makeba, they told me. Until now I'd never even heard of her."

"Ah, Makeba," he said. "I don't know if I admire her more for her voice or her courage. We have a lot to learn from that remarkable woman." He stood the bowl on a table and for a moment rested his arms around the young couple's shoulders. It was a portrait, not of a father and daughter and her fiancé, but of good friends.

The house stood at the top of an eroded fold in the hills. Around us the wilderness withered under the merciless sun. While "the kids" blended the berries into the cream, Hutchins and I sat in deck chairs, in the shade of the jacarandas, looking down the canyon. At first, I think, we simply talked about the savage majesty of the Santa Barbara mountains; but before long, I remember, the conversation turned to education.

When I admitted that I knew very little about the "great books," it was the classicist in Hutchins who replied. He spoke like a medieval physician. The books, he explained, are an emulsion of wisdom and knowledge laced with useful information. They're like medicine, he said, for the afflicted mind and the wounded spirit in any age.

"You must be disappointed, then, that your daughter left St. John's for a junior college."

He turned to me and smiled. "Not at all! I think it's the smartest thing she's ever done." I didn't respond, because I didn't know what to say. His smile broadened. "You seem surprised."

Above us a hawk, motionless on its thermal perch, repeated a wavering cry, then, dipping one wing, wheeled in a slow circle. Hutchins looked up and watched it before he spoke again. Finally he said, "You see, the community college is the last hope for American higher education." He turned to me, not smiling now. "I think that surprises you, too."

I asked if his advocacy of both St. John's and the community college wasn't anomalous. Wasn't the community college the antithesis of St. John's? His reply was deliberate and eloquent. I no longer recall his exact words, but in essence he said, no, both institutions are indispensable to a democratic society. The "great books" are there. They are as available and immutable as Polaris for fixing the course of democracy. The community college is, in part, a product of the "great books." Its commitment to taking any student, regardless of age or prior preparation, from where he is to somewhere beyond fulfills an historical imperative. Then he said something that sounded familiar: "It used to be that only the privileged went to school. Now everyone can be educated. But a lot of students, old and young alike—my daughter, for one—will just drop out of school if they're subjected to a rusty, creaking curriculum. The junior college is the remedy for that."

I made a remark that I intended to be humorous; but as soon as I spoke, I was afraid it sounded sarcastic: "What you're saying is, 'From each according to his abilities, to each according to his needs.'"

His eyes narrowed in sly amusement. "You'd better not let our friends in the John Birch Society hear you say that. But, yes, that's the truth."

For a time neither of us said anything more. Overhead the sky was as blank and colorless as sheet metal. The hawk had slid from sight. Suddenly imagining that Hutchins' exaltation of the two-year college might have been a subtle indictment of my own teaching, I started talking to him as if he were my father, too. "You know, I don't think I'm really cut out to be a teacher." He looked bemused. "No? My daughter seems to think you are."

I was about to tell him that my students didn't understand my lectures about "descriptive grammar" or logical positivism; but as if he already knew what I was going to say, he went on: "Maybe you stimulate wonder in your students. That's all a teacher really needs to do."

"But they don't remember anything that I tell them." Even to me it sounded like a whine.

He brushed the air with his hand. Sternly, but not unkindly, he said, "What they remember isn't that important!" He waited a few seconds, and then, more gently, he said, "Teaching is a license to enter your students' lives. In my experience, a nineteen-year-old will often tell his teacher things about himself that he wouldn't, or couldn't, even tell his parents. Your job is to help him be himself, plainspoken and completely honest." He paused again and looked down at his open palms. "And to help him avoid the trap of his own history and background."

We were silent for another several minutes. I stared down the canyon. Ribbed and the color of bone, it looked like a giant skeleton bleaching in the sun.

Finally Hutchins spoke. "Anyway, I know my daughter trusts you. She may not always understand you, but she believes that you mean to help her. What do you think of that?"

"What I'm thinking about is resigning in June."

He fixed me in his blue gaze. "That's too bad," he said. I believed he meant it.

Then, in a very loud voice, but as if it were still part of our conversation, he said, "I was told we were having strawberry ice cream this afternoon, weren't you?"

One day soon after my conversation with Hutchins, a student in a composition class vigorously protested an assignment. "Why do we have to learn to write, anyway?" he demanded.

"Because someday, maybe, you'll have something you want to say, and you'll have the skills to say it." The orthodox retort. Recalling Hutchins' words, I added, "Trust me."

I don't remember the young man's name now, nor do I recall the exact topic; but it was no doubt characteristic of assignments found in textbooks of the time: "From a current magazine, choose two advertisements for similar products (for example, automobiles). Using the crite-

ria established in the preceding essay, compare and contrast the advertisements. Include in your discussion [. . .]."

The student remarked dryly that he didn't think he'd want to say
things like that someday.

Later, still bothered by the student's objections, I tried, as we often
do after a confrontation, to salve the sting by reviewing all the things "I
should have said." But something odd happened. The harder I tried to
rationalize the assignment and justify my response to the student, the
deeper the stain of doubt that spread across my thinking.

At first I merely conceded that the student was right about the assignment, that he wasn't likely to want to say things like that someday. Then
it occurred to me that maybe writing assignments didn't teach writing
skills at all, but cynicism and irresponsibility.

For a few minutes I leaned back, locking my hands behind my head.
Wryly I recalled the many meaningless papers that I'd had to write in
school. I saw that assignments were routinely used as snares. Told to
write on subjects that neither engaged nor illumined them, students were
forced to contrive indifferent, poorly crafted papers that mandated harsh
criticism and low grades from their teachers.

Over the racket of my thoughts I could still hear Hutchins' words,
plain and elemental as birdsong: "Given traditional instruction, these
kids will just drop out of school."

Half an hour later I had concluded that even the term "writing assignment" was an insidious oxymoron. If he was told what to write, and usually how to write it, a student couldn't be expected to write plainly and
honestly. It was "obedience training," not learning.

Though from this distance the idea seems so self-evident that it ought
to be preceded by the phrase "needless to say," at the time I thought I'd
been struck by revelation.

By the next class session the young man still hadn't started to work
on his paper. "Walk with me," I said after class. "I want to talk to you."
I asked him to tell me about himself, about his interests, his aspirations,
even, if he wanted, his frustrations and disappointments. Enter your students' lives, Hutchins had said.

His father, the student told me, was an internationally known race-
car driver who had competed in the Indianapolis 500. Someday, he, too,
would compete in the Indy. He knew all about cars, he said. He worked
in an auto body shop, and on his own he rebuilt car engines, "souped
them up." He hadn't really objected to writing, and certainly not to writing about cars; it was writing about advertisements for cars that he had
found stultifying. Suddenly, even before we reached my office, he
assigned himself a paper: He would compare the racing capabilities of
Ford and Chevy stock cars.

After that day, I remember, I raced through the few weeks remaining in the semester as though running through a house switching lights on in every room. At last I turned my back on The Great Vowel Shift and The Noble Savage and for the first time came face-to-face with the students in front of me.

Seeing my experience with the car enthusiast as a precedent, I set about undoing what I now perceived as the dual deterrents to writing development: assigned topics and grades. I met with students one-by-one, and while getting to know them, worked with them on ideas for their next papers. As for grading, if I were honestly handing the responsibility for their writing to the students themselves, then I had relinquished my authority to say that some papers "failed" or that one was "better" than another. My obligation, I decided, was to evaluate how well a student's writing developed over time; for now, I would respond to individual papers strictly with comments and suggestions for revision. "From each according to his abilities, to each according to his needs."

At about the same time, I recognized that the handbook we'd been using was intended more to preserve a writing mystique than to provide students with realistic skills. It was witch-doctor pedagogy: Wearing an amulet of sticks and bones would be as felicitous to a student's writing abilities as ritually following the procedures prescribed in the text. At best, the book reduced writing to little more than filling out a questionnaire. At worst, it nourished a lie: What we call "composition," the book implied, is purely form; content is irrelevant. Once form is mastered, it can be filled like a bottle with any material. Remembering Hutchins' words, "Your job is to help students be themselves, to take control of their lives," I abandoned the text.

I continued to struggle with the question "Why do we have to learn to write, anyway?" as if it were an unsolved riddle. Then, one afternoon as I idly thought about old movies, it occurred to me that maybe film and writing were invented for the same reason: to satisfy the human urge to share the pictures generated and stored in our heads. If that were the case, I reasoned, description, conveying concrete images, was not just one type of writing, as the handbook suggested, but the basic element of all writing.

Following the hunch, I introduced a new exercise. Every day someone in the class would choose a subject, an item or an action, or a person in the room at the time, and for ten minutes we would all describe what we saw, writing constantly, not stopping to think. "This isn't composition, mind you," I told the class. "It's a warm-up for composition, a daily workout of bends and stretches to keep your writing in shape." Although we were all presumably describing the same thing, I discovered that our descriptions differed substantially. At last I had partially solved the riddle. "That's one reason for learning to write," I told the class. "Because no one else sees things exactly the way you do."

And so it went during those final weeks of the semester. One realization led to another, at an accelerating pace, as though insight were subject to some fundamental law of physics. Then, abruptly, the semester was over.

After the last meeting of my nine o'clock class, I crossed the quad toward my office, thinking once again about things "I should have said." Deconstruction of my own classes was becoming a habit. Already the sun of summer held the city hostage. I took refuge in the shade of the pepper tree, another habit, and looked up to see Robert Hutchins' daughter.

"Ah, Miss Hutchins."

For a minute neither of us spoke, as though now that the class was over, there was nothing more to be said. Finally, I spoke. "I think I've been very lucky this semester. I'm glad you took a chance on my class. And I'm grateful for the good fortune of having met your father."

She smiled and tipped her head to one side, and I thought she was going to make some reciprocal remark. But the blue of her eyes turned smoky, like her father's when he looked inward. She reached out and we shook hands. I watched her as she crossed the lawn. As I watched, I thought of the afternoon on the Hutchins' terrace. I remembered that as we ate our ice cream we had talked about Karl Jung and the concept of synchronicity. "All a part of a plan," I said, grinning, then looked around to see if anyone had heard me talking to myself. Finally I ventured out from the sheltering shade.

On another hot morning, two or three years later, an orange flame blossomed in the dry brush below the Hutchins terrace then another, and another. Within minutes, the canyon, like a flue, had drawn the fire up into the house. Before firefighters could get there, the house and all of Hutchins' books and manuscripts, his diaries and journals, were ash, and the wilderness had reclaimed the terrace.

By then I had left Santa Barbara for a position at the College of San Mateo. There, acceding to destiny, I continued to teach composition, as well as screenwriting and film production, for three decades. In 1971, almost at the midpoint in my career, I read in the paper that Robert Hutchins had died; but I'd carried his words with me, a greater prize than the "great books" themselves.

On a dreary sodden afternoon recently, going through my mail, I opened a letter from a man who said he had studied at the College of San Mateo in the late 1980s. He had been enrolled in two of my classes, he said.

"You probably don't remember me," he wrote, "but maybe you remember a project I submitted in a filmmaking class. In my film I performed, in costume, the final scene from the opera *Pagliacci*. For my soundtrack I used Enrico Caruso's recording."

I clearly remembered his tortured clown and knew at once who he was. I also recalled, though, that I used to worry that he was an academic drifter, and I remembered that he enrolled in classes randomly and only sporadically. Eventually he had disappeared entirely, perhaps one of those students who "simply lose interest and drop out of school altogether." But after all, I thought, hadn't my own course work often been random and unfocused?

I took up his letter again. "When I left San Mateo, still not sure of what I wanted to do with my life, I went to Europe, ultimately working in Paris as an *au pair* because I wanted to learn French. These days I design furniture, and I have a lot I want to say about art, design, aesthetics, and even architecture. I've written a number of articles on these subjects, and since I've never forgotten how supportive and encouraging you were, I wonder if we could meet sometime so that I could show you what I've written. Maybe you could even suggest someplace I could send my articles to be published."

I switched on the desk lamp and looked out the window. The rain had stopped, glazing the street in twilight. I sat for a time thumbing the yellowed pages of memory. Hutchins spoke: "Your job is to help a student to be himself," he said. I reflected on how those of us who taught in the two-year college had done our job well while literally making our own way in the profession. Hutchins spoke again: "The community college is the hope of higher education," he said, and just then I caught sight of myself smiling back from the darkening pane.

# 5

# Evolution of a Writing Program

## Barbara Stout

## Introduction

When good luck brought me in 1971 to the English department at Montgomery College in Maryland, I knew a few things. I knew that I wanted to teach at a college or university and that my experience as an adjunct had confirmed this choice and let me work out some of the beginner's wobbles. I also knew that composition was a required course but that literature was what we thought about and read about and talked about. I did not know anything about community colleges as institutions, and I had never heard of composition or rhetoric as disciplines worthy of scholarly attention.

But fortunately, four forces worked together during those early years to help me understand the mission and culture of community colleges, to inspire a commitment to composition and, simultaneously, to bring changes to the composition program at Montgomery College. The forces were, first, student demographics and needs; second, mentoring and leadership from colleagues; third, the work of organizations, especially the Conference on College Composition and Communication, the Northeast Conference on English in the Two-Year College (now Two-Year College English Association (TYCA)-Northeast), National TYCA, the Community College Humanities Association (CCHA), and the National Writing Project; and fourth, new and revised textbooks.

Montgomery College (MC) was founded in 1946, and like most community colleges, it has experienced increases in enrollment and in student diversity during every decade of its history. During the thirty years from 1971 to 2001, demographic shifts clearly mandated some of the changes that I describe in this essay. In 1971, 9,535 students enrolled; in 2001, there were 21,347. In 1971, the only categories by which students were identified were gender and county, state, or out-of-state residential status. In 1975, racial identities were first recorded and "International Students" became a category. In that year, 10 percent of MC's students were international, 6 percent black, 1 percent Hispanic, and 0 percent Asian. In 2001, 34 percent of the students were identified as "non U.S."; 27 percent were black; 13 percent were Hispanic; 16 percent were Asian. (The "non U.S." students were counted both as a single category and within racial groups.) "White" students went from 80 percent in 1975 to 43 percent in 2001. The gender numbers flip-flopped from 57 percent male/43 percent female in 1971 to 57 percent female/43 percent male in 2001. In addition, the average student age moved up from 23 to 28.

Also, in these years, the profession of English was gloriously active, and many faculty at Montgomery College and in its region were involved. I can't name all the colleagues who led me and our college, but I want to cite a few. The fields in which these friends labor are central to community college composition programs because of their common push toward inclusiveness and the spread of higher literacy. At Montgomery: Myrna Goldenberg, feminism, multiculturalism, humanities issues, and Holocaust scholarship; Suzanne Liggett, computers and composition; Dianne Ganz Scheper, honors programs and humanities; Carolyn Chism and Evelyn Elder, developmental programs; Christine McMahon, critical literacy; at Prince George's Community College: Anne King, writing across the curriculum; at Howard University, Eleanor Traylor, African American studies and narratology; at Catholic University, Rosemary Winslow, the Writing Project and composition; at the University of Maryland, Jeanne Fahnestock, rhetoric; at Old Dominion University, Joyce Neff, WAC and composition; and in Baltimore, Barbara Walvoord and the Baltimore Area Consortium for Writing across the Curriculum, fondly known as BACWAC.

The work that these colleagues did and continue to do in composition, developmental writing, rhetoric, computers, and WAC is obviously connected with changes in the composition program. However, their efforts in multicultural and feminist scholarship and their commitment to substantial, humanistic content have also informed the curriculum shifts that we have made at MC, keeping us focused on human reasons for responsible communication and reminding us of the necessity of inclusion with transition and achievement.

## Changes (and Consistencies) in a Composition Program

In 1971, within the English department we had a two-semester composition sequence, one "review" (remedial) course, a single, all-purpose ESL course, and two remedial reading courses, along with a healthy variety of literature courses. Now, a four-level ESL sequence and a redesigned reading program are in another department because the growth of all programs made it difficult to administer them in one unit. A technical writing course was added and then revised and expanded into several offerings. The literature program has changed, too, with more inclusive readings in all courses. Although all these changes merit full description, I'm going to describe here only the composition sequence and the developmental writing program for native speakers.

But before I get to changes, I'm happy to report that some things have not varied. First of all, both the 1971 and the 2001 programs were developed by thoughtful faculty, knowledgeable about the professional issues of their times and concerned with what they thought college writers should be able to do. We still have a program designed by faculty committees and then voted on by the department faculty. We still have agreed-upon departmental syllabi, with clearly stated basic requirements that are applied to faculty evaluation as well as to student grades. We still have two semesters of composition, which we believe most community college students need. The syllabi, in 1971 and currently, emphasize the production of well-organized papers, basic concepts of rhetoric, analysis of a variety of readings, and undergraduate-level researched writing. Then and now, grading standards reflect a conviction that college writers must be able to produce conventionally acceptable, adult-level finished texts. And—bless you, founders—central to the courses, then and now, is a required folder in which a student must keep course work (yes, a kind of portfolio).

Established in the 1950s, the Montgomery College Composition Folder is central to writing instruction and to both student and faculty evaluation. No-nonsense instructions printed on the front tell students that they must maintain their folders and hand them in at the end of the semester to pass the course. They also state that finished versions of syllabi-mandated assignments must be in the folder—revised, corrected, identified, fastened in, and listed on the conveniently provided space inside the cover. Beyond the somewhat hickory-stick virtue of discipline, keeping the folder encourages students to respect their own writing, take responsibility for their work, and pride in its presentation. And, of course, it's useful for faculty to see a student's entire semester's work instead of only a series of squiggles in a grade book! Faculty usually collect these folders at midterm and ask students to bring them to conferences, procedures worked out many years before the portfolio movement became popular in the early 1990s.

As the major component of a performance evaluation, faculty must give the department's evaluation committee several student folders illustrating the full range of grades, along with instructional materials and student evaluations. Adjunct and junior faculty have to turn in more folders than senior faculty, but we all do it for every evaluation no matter how long we've been teaching or how good our reputations. They provide a snapshot of much that goes on in a composition class. Faculty presenting student folders experience similar kinds of respect, responsibility, pride, and nervousness as do students handing in folders.

Three decades ago, an EN 101 student wrote at least eight "themes," on whatever topics an instructor assigned. These "themes" had to be based on the traditional organizational patterns, such as process and comparison/contrast. Outlines were sanctified, with a possible preference for "sentence" outlines over "topic" outlines. Sentence fragments were sinful (still are, sometimes), and comma splices led to perdition (still do, sometimes). Response was heavily error based; many called it "correcting." *The Harbrace College Handbook*, which then started with a chapter on parts of speech, ruled. Our program was a living example of what some scholars have labeled the "current/traditional" approach.

I remember knowing, thirty years ago, that the students' folders would be central to my evaluation and that I'd better demonstrate my ability to correct a lot of errors. (Now, my peers evaluate the entire writing process as well as the soundness of the grades.) I remember nervously wondering, thirty years ago, if it would be okay to set aside class time for conferences, and being told that a cautious amount would be all right. I'm sure that I did most of the talking in those early conferences and that I edited students' "rough" drafts heavily, not understanding how to be a writing coach. I remember that I occasionally had students exchange papers and comment on what a classmate had done. Now, of course, my students work in class with drafts at all stages—with me and with each other in various configurations.

## Some Changes

As in my own classes, some changes in our program are more pedagogical than substantial, though assignments have changed and readings reflect ethnicities and genders that didn't get much attention in 1971. The current EN 101 students write fewer finished papers, a minimum of four; they do in-class writing, now distinguished from writing done over time; they work through drafts and revisions of their papers; they write summaries and outlines of readings; learn reasons for citation of sources, not just formats; complete a self-paced library workbook and a course-wide exam. Instructors help students to understand their own writing processes, and many require some kind of journal or other informal writing. Clearly, such practices are typical of those used across the country.

In the 1980s we developed an expanded version of EN 101, labeled EN 101A, for ESL students and others who can benefit from extra class time. EN 101A provides five hours of class time, for which students pay tuition, and three hours of graduation and transfer credit. Faculty provide individual and group attention to students' needs with drafts, revisions, punctuation, formats, and grammar.

The second-semester course, with a double focus on research and rhetoric, has changed little. However, the syllabus now uses the phrase "research project," which culminates in a paper, rather than talks about *the* research paper. And there is much more emphasis on understanding argument as bringing agreement, rather than as a means of conquest.

In 1976, the Writing Center was established on the Rockville Campus. Open to all students, it primarily serves those in ESL, developmental, or credit composition courses. Full-time and adjunct faculty do the tutoring. Like many colleges, we began to add computers in the mid-1980s, and the Writing Center now offers individual and networked connectivity.

## Developmental Writing

Since 1971, the developmental program has changed a great deal in its structure, though not in its primary goal, which is to help native speakers of English. In 1971, the course was called Review English, and its syllabus shouted "grammar," with its focus on first, nouns, then verbs, adjectives, adverbs, all the way to phrases, clauses, paragraphs, and essays. Uncomfortable with this approach, I furtively taught according to my own philosophy, hoping that the senior faculty would not notice. My students wrote paragraphs and short essays, before and after our engagement with nouns, verbs, adjectives, etc. We analyzed their own sentences as well as those in the required workbook.

Native and nonnative speakers of English took the same developmental class because the ESL program had not yet expanded beyond a one-semester course. Further, in an effort to be fully open in admissions policies, the college administration eliminated required placement testing in the early 1970s, so fewer and fewer native speakers enrolled in Review English, no matter their needs.

Within a few years, however, healthy changes came about, driven by student demographics and faculty insights. First of all, the college developed programs for speakers of other languages and for disabled students, including those with learning disabilities, so they were no longer inappropriately included in the single "review" course. Then composition, reading, and counseling faculty developed a Basic English program that we continue to refine. This developmental program has much in common with those at community colleges across the country.

The assessment testing for entering students that was dropped in the 1970s was reestablished in steps over several years and is now strictly administered. Students must enroll in appropriate basic writing and reading courses as indicated by English and reading scores, academic records, and advising information. Like many colleges, Montgomery provides two sequenced courses, each of which concentrates on writing short essays, both personal and reading-based, with sentence-level concerns firmly addressed in context. Students in Basic English I may pass into English 101 or 101A without taking Basic English II by fulfilling specific course requirements and passing uniform Essay Competence Exams and Objective Competency Exams designed and administered by faculty. An additional component, called Pathways, focuses on reading and includes counseling to help students find the paths that will lead to success in college.

The move from one grammar-heavy course in the early 1970s to Basic English I, Basic English II, accompanying reading courses, and Pathways marks the biggest change that thirty years have brought to Montgomery's English program, and it also reflects the profession's changing focus on student needs.

# Testing

Assessment testing for entering students was reestablished through administrative and faculty efforts. In addition, after years of meetings, faculty and administrators at all of Maryland's community colleges reached agreement on statewide consistency in scores for entry into credit-level composition courses. Further, at Montgomery, there is now a required examination in the first-semester composition course. In 1971, such testing was not part of the program.

A major change in the program was the addition in 1993 of the EN 101 "competency exam," which students must pass. It is a typical written-to-a-prompt, holistically scored essay. Our debates about adopting such a test went on for many years until, eventually, we voted in favor of it, relying heavily on Edward White's work and ETS as we set it up. With Edward White's help, we have evaluated the exam, and a faculty committee has recently refined it.

Here's another place where I changed. When this kind of exam was proposed over a decade ago, I opposed it because I did not want such heavy weight placed on a spontaneously written argumentative essay. After we tried the test, however, I became a fervent convert, convinced that all college students should be able to write a reasonably proficient short response to a question within a specific interval of time. Moreover, the students take the test very seriously; the weight of the exam forces them to work on their writing hard enough to pass it. Anonymous readers can't be charmed or urged to pity, and no one else can write for a student (although we've had a few imaginative attempts). And the exam increases consistency in a large program spanning three campuses, with about seventy full-time faculty and ninety adjuncts, many of whom are new each semester.

One bonus was unexpected. The competency exam revealed that many inexperienced instructors were giving decent grades to plagiarized work. The plagiarism appeared largely inadvertent, making us newly alert to the need for greatly improved instruction in the use of sources, with more emphasis on the integration of voices than on the mechanics of formats. We've discussed this subject in meetings with adjuncts—and with new full-time faculty—and in the adjunct newsletter.

## Writing-Across-the-Curriculum/Critical Literacy

Montgomery College's WAC story is not unusual, either. Like many colleges, we established a Writing-Across-the-Curriculum program in the mid-1980s, using the common faculty workshop approach and relying on missionary-type enthusiasm, hopes by a few that some magic might transform student writing, and a modest budget. A gratifying number of faculty from many disciplines participated in events focusing on writing as a means of learning, expanding the assignment repertoire, designing assignments, and responding to student writing. We tried to resolve some of the impediments to WAC that are inherent to community colleges: the spectrum of abilities among an open-admissions student body, the absence of upper-division courses and students, heavy teaching loads, employed students, and many part-time faculty.

About eight years ago, WAC expanded into Critical Literacy, inspired by a program at Oakton Community College in Illinois. For several years, the Critical Literacy Program provided yearlong faculty seminars for selected instructors who committed themselves to revising a course to include more writing, critical thinking, and critical reading. Now, the Critical Literacy Committee provides workshops for new faculty to help them emphasize effective writing, thinking, and reading in their courses.

## Conclusion

I wish I could say that Montgomery College's program is a model. Of course, I think it's sound, and, of course, I try to teach what I believe is ideal. This retrospective analysis leads me to conclude that most of the changes of the last thirty-plus years in our two-year-college writing program have been positive. Virtually every change occurred because of intense interest on the faculty's part providing the best instruction for students. The forces that brought about changes in Montgomery College's writing program are still at work and will, of course, bring more changes. The history of its writing program is reflective of the evolutionary efforts of many two-year colleges to serve their students most effectively, and in the process, allow faculty to develop professionally as teacher-scholars.

## Works Cited

White, E. M. 1989. *Developing Successful College Writing Programs*. San Francisco: Jossey.

———. 1994. *Teaching and Assessing Writing*. 2nd ed. San Francisco: Jossey.

# 6

## Lessons from a Cactus:
## Divergent Teaching in a Converging World

### William V. Costanzo

When people ask me about the unprecedented growth of two-year colleges and their curricula, I often think of a plant that someone gave me for my office. It was a cactus: a fleshy, green globe in a shallow pot. Over the years, the cactus sprouted many smaller nodes. With richer soil and brighter sunlight, it might have nurtured longer roots and grown into a single, robust barrel cactus. But left to itself, it spread laterally, branching out in several directions, much like my career. If I had taught at a four-year school attached to a university, like the one from which I earned my Ph.D., I most likely would have become a specialist, focusing most of my teaching and research on a single topic such as Restoration drama or James Joyce. Instead, I wound up at an institution where the terrain was boundless, if not deep. I found myself teaching and writing about topics as diverse as Joseph Conrad and laser discs, basic writing and TV commercials, filmmaking and computer programming. And in each case, it was my students who pointed the way.

For it was clear to me in 1970, when I taught my first students at Westchester Community College in Valhalla, New York, that I was not going to do unto them what had been done to me. I was not going to deliver lectures and assign term papers and let them guess what would be on the final exam. If I were to be honest, if I were really interested in their education, I knew I had to do most of the listening. And what I heard was that these students came from very different backgrounds. After leaving my class, they returned to lives and expectations that were worlds away from the classroom as I knew it. Many were juggling their coursework with jobs and family responsibilities. Some returned to neighborhoods where higher education was a foreign culture or where English was a second language. I began to realize that their assumptions about reading, writing, and learning were divided from mine by a cultural gap.

There was a lesson here in cultural literacy. In the late 1980s, when E. D. Hirsch was proposing to identify the core knowledge needed by a literate adult, he based his "national literate vocabulary" largely on a print-oriented, Western tradition, from Achilles to Zola. I realized that I had mastered much of this lexicon through many years of reading classics of the academic canon. How could my students, few of whom were schooled in the Great Books, expect to acquire such fluency in reading and writing while commuting between the campus and their varied lives? And how could I expect to help them attain Hirsch's standards of literacy in the brief time I had them in my classes?

Listening to their talk, however, made me question Hirsch's premise. For if their daily discourse made no reference to Laocoön or Leda and the swan, it did allude quite deftly to Darth Vader, Oprah, MTV, the Energizer bunny, gangsta' rap, and an impressive range of other terms drawn from popular culture. I began to realize that their knowledge of the popular media formed a frame of reference for a distinctive form of literacy, what has come to be known as media literacy. *Media literacy* is defined as the ability to produce and understand messages in a variety of media, including television, film, and radio as well as print. As a teacher, I wondered how this framework might serve as the basis for a new curriculum, one that might enlarge the teaching of English to embrace the richness of popular culture. I wondered, for example, how studying movies might complement the study of written literature. I wondered whether filmmaking might be understood and practiced as a form of composition, reinforcing skills and concepts common to both film production and writing. I wondered if the mental activities needed to make sense of a commercial or a television news program were similar to those required to read a persuasive essay or a research paper. In short, I began to seek connections between the academic task for which I had been hired and the larger worlds to which my students belonged.

My formal education had given me scant preparation for this kind of work. I was well versed in English literature from the Middle Ages to the modernists (as modern as James Joyce and T. S. Eliot). I was well trained to do close readings of texts by disciples of the New Critics (as new as R. P. Blackmur and John Crowe Ransom). But I knew nothing of reader response theory or the research on composing. I had never taken a film course or seen a television in a classroom. And about computers, I knew absolutely nothing. Nor did most of my colleagues. We learned about media and technology, about audience response and the composing process, as our field evolved, following the felt needs of our students and our own branching interests.

The two-year college offered a healthy climate for this kind of growth. Without the pressure to publish a body of "significant research," we could concentrate on teaching. Without the academic walls of specialization, we were free to range in other fields. For example, I was free to teach a course called Fiction into Film, in which students learned about literature by turning short stories into movies. I could wheel a television monitor into my freshman composition class to study the organizing strategies of commercials. A Title III grant enabled me and other faculty to build a computer-equipped writing lab to test the benefits and risks of electronic texts. Because our students were nontraditional, we were encouraged to explore nontraditional alternatives to traditional teaching methods and materials.

Much of this exploring was piecemeal and intuitive. We were guided by a sense of possibility shaped by student response. If an idea worked well in the classroom, we added it to our bag of tricks. Gradually, as we assembled a repertoire of successful practices, we began to look for a guiding philosophy. Why did these tricks work? How might they be connected into a consistent pedagogy supported by sound theories and research?

The most important concepts in our field evolved along such lines of inquiry. Listening in the 1970s to Janet Emig speak about the composing processes of twelfth graders or to Mina Shaughnessey talk about the errors and expectations of basic writers, I learned the importance of listening to students. Instead of recirculating the received wisdom passed on by my college teachers, I saw that a two-year-college classroom could be an open field for fresh research. If we teachers kept an open mind and watched how our students learned instead of trying to fill their minds with precepts, we might learn how writers really write and readers really read. The best research on the composing process and reader response began with this approach.

A course called Film as Composition followed a similar path. I had bought a Super-8 camera in 1969 and noticed that the steps I took to make a film were much like those I followed to write an essay. Filmmakers, like writers, must choose to focus on a subject, explore it from different angles, look for patterns, edit what they find, arrange their findings into a sequence linked by transitions and a guiding purpose, revise it for an audience, and so on. When I brought my camera to class and invited my students to make a movie on the subjects they were writing about, I noticed several things. Predictably, their enthusiasm for the project rose, partly from the novelty of using cameras, partly through the synergy of collaborative effort, partly because the final product would be a screening for their peers, not just an essay for the teacher. More important, though, was what they learned about the process of composing. Because filmmaking is a more visual process than writing, the choices were often easier to see. With a camera, they could move closer to a subject to focus on details or change the angle to achieve a different point of view; whereas, when they were writing, concepts such as framing, focus, and point of view seemed more abstract. It was easier to visualize the options of editing when they were cutting lengths of film and rearranging them on pins than when they were moving words around in their heads.

A modest grant from the National Endowment for the Humanities in 1978 helped me to pursue the analogy of film as composition through classroom practice and research. I studied the methods of documentary filmmakers. I consulted the literature on reading and semiotics to compare the English language and the language of film as symbol systems. I referred to the work of cognitive scientists and neurophysiologists to learn how visual and verbal information is processed in the brain. I read cultural histories to understand writing, film, and television as developments in human communication. My findings, published in the book *Double Exposure*, served to support a curriculum for first-year college English that draws on students' simultaneous exposure to two complementary forms of composition: visual and verbal. It is a curriculum that I have been building with my students ever since.

Meanwhile, my approach to literature was taking the form of Fiction into Film. It was a course based on the premise that, for many of today's students, film, television, and video have assumed the storytelling functions of written literature. My original purpose was to use filmmaking as a bridge to literature. Working in production groups, students selected a promising short story to adapt for the screen. They learned how to operate a camera, light a set, direct actors, and edit footage. They studied the art of screenwriting and created storyboards to work out the visual appearance of their story. In the process, they became more careful, appreciative readers of literary texts. More than ever before, they paid attention to the elements of fiction because they had to translate those elements into cinematic terms. In order to cast the actors, scout locations, or choose a camera setup, they had to study characterization, setting, and point of view. For the first time, I saw many of my students reading fiction with a resolute and steady purpose: marking certain passages, analyzing their construction, rereading them with an eye for the telling details. They were also developing a critical vocabulary and evaluative criteria because, in order to convince their classmates to film their favorite works, they needed words and arguments to make their case. The payoff was both an original movie at the end of the course and an enduring, insider's understanding of what goes into a work of literature.

Later on, as film gained widespread acceptance as an academic course of study, I began to see myself as a teacher and scholar of both literature and film. I took an NEH Summer Seminar on film study with Peter Brunette in 1983, joined the Society for Cinema Studies, and began presenting and publishing my work on cinema. I was invited to direct NCTE's Commission on Media and to join the scholarly advisory board for a ten-part series on American Cinema that was broadcast on national public television. My participation in the American Cinema Project prepared me to write a book for other English teachers interested in film, entitled *Reading the Movies* in 1992, followed by a sequel, *Great Films and How to Teach Them*, in 2004. Such projects might have diverted my attention from the classroom at another institution, but at Westchester Community College, I found that it was always possible to sow back into teaching the seeds of my scholarship and research. American Cinema became a course that I still teach, expanding it each year as I grow with the profession.

Meanwhile, it gradually grew clear that my efforts were part of something larger. It is sometimes difficult to recognize that local eddies of activity are flowing parallel to other currents or to know when their combined momentum has reached the scope and power of a movement. But by the mid-1980s, I realized that my colleagues and I were in the middle of a national movement for media education. The perception began at local, state, and national conferences where like-minded teachers met to talk about their experiences with film and television in the English classroom. It grew stronger when those teachers formed committees and gave workshops on visual media under the auspices of established organizations, then established subgroups or organizations of their own. It grew stronger still when they contributed articles to professional publications or launched new publications. With each step, what once seemed marginal and fragmented became more central and whole.

The chronology of my consolidating efforts began within the National Council of Teachers of English. I first joined the Commission on Media in 1983, chairing a special Committee on Film Study during the next three years and helping to form a new Assembly on Media Arts for the rank and file in 1990. The Assembly planned a series of national conferences focusing on media education, eventually migrating from the East Coast (Philadelphia in 1992) through the Mid-West (Madison, Wisconsin, in 1994) to the West (San Jose, California, in 1998). Meanwhile, we allied ourselves with groups such as the National Telemedia Council, the National Alliance of Media Arts & Culture, Strategies for Media Literacy, and the Association for Media Literacy in Canada. I found myself invited to places beyond the routine boundaries of academia, like the Aspen Institute (in 1992) and the President's Office of Drug Control Policy (in 1995), to discuss the future of media education. The movement was taking hold.

In a cultural environment more broadly viewed than the one defined by E. D. Hirsch, it was natural for my lifelong interest in literature and writing to expand into the parallel fields of cinema and media studies. Less predictable was the alliance between composition and computers that has by now become a regular feature of the English curriculum. Two-year colleges were among the first to recognize the special value of computers for the nontraditional students that they serve. Computer-assisted writing seemed to make the most difference for inexperienced and reluctant writers. The blinking screen kept their attention longer than the blank inertness of the page. The keyboard and spelling checker helped to bypass certain learning problems. Built-in prewriting and revision aids rendered the otherwise mysterious options of writing as visible as pulldown menus and as convenient as special function keys.

At nearby LaGuardia Community College, Brian Gallagher had outfitted a classroom with Apple II computers for students with certified learning disabilities. In the early 1980s, Professor Gallagher was among the first to recognize how many of their disabilities were reduced when the keyboard and the screen replaced pen and paper. Elsewhere, classroom teachers were experimenting with software for the language arts. Distressed by the growth of routine drill and practice programs, they realized that even English teachers could learn a programming language well enough to create their own software, software that supported more productive methodologies. In 1984, Hugh Burns invented *TOPOI*, which offered student writers a series of questions to help explore their topics systematically. Burns' work ushered in a generation of prewriting tools, including James Strickland's *QUEST* and Helen Schwartz's *SEEN*. Meanwhile, other tools were being developed to help students with revision. At Colorado State University, Dawn Rodrigues used *Writer's Workbench* (first developed at Bell Labs) to help her students analyze their compositions. *Writer's Workbench* gave them information about sentence length, structure, verb choice, and punctuation. It also flagged certain spelling errors. A more flexible and comprehensive set of writing tools was developed by William Wresch, a teacher of English and computer science at the University of Wisconsin. His *Writer's Helper* offered basic word processing with menus for prewriting (brainstorming, freewriting, questions for exploring topics), drafting (outlining, common organizing patterns), and revision (text analysis for sentence length, transitions, readability), putting what our profession was learning about the composing process within easy reach.

My own inquiry into the culture of computers started with some observations in my classes. By the mid-1980s, some of these classes were meeting in a classroom equipped with Apple II computers acquired through a federal grant. I noticed that when I typed a literature assignment on a word processor and the students read it on the screen, they paid closer attention to the details. If I left spaces for their responses

between my questions, they would scroll carefully through the assignment, answering each question more thoroughly than they had ever done
on my painstakingly detailed handouts. This was good news. My questions grew more ambitious. I added writing tips and definitions of literary terms. I even learned the BASIC programming language so I could
present questions one screen at a time, offering students a way to write
and print out their responses from the keyboard. I had created my first
computer program.

As computer technology advanced, as Pentiums replaced the Apple
IIs, I recast the program using windows, pull-down menus, file options,
and other features to make it more convenient. I also augmented the traditional pedagogy of literary analysis with ideas drawn from reader
response theory. The program, now called *Literature Tutor*, has become
an interactive primer for analyzing fiction, guiding students through the
task of literary study with explanations, questions, critical tools, and
other forms of help along the way. Revising *Literature Tutor* over the
years—deciding what to include, watching how students respond to my
words on the screen, sharpening the language and fine-tuning key ideas—
has taught me more about teaching and learning literature than nearly
any other faculty development activity.

Meanwhile, like many of my colleagues, I watched a new generation
grow up with computers. Young people who had come through childhood
with computer games were trading in their joysticks for a keyboard, learning to use the computer as a writing instrument, a research tool, an art
studio, and a science lab. I realized that the computer was not just a tool,
but an environment, and that it was shaping the way many people were
learning to read, write, and reason. I wanted to learn along with them,
delving deeper into the technology of microchips, the art of programming,
the promises and perils of word processing, hypertext, and artificial intelligence, publishing what I learned in *The Electronic Text* in 1989.

What I learned is that the computer is more than a delivery system,
more than a convenient tool; it is the language environment in which
more and more of our thinking and communicating takes place. What it
adds to other media, such as books and films, is the capacity for interaction. The computer draws readers into the text, inviting them to make
decisions. As readers, they decide which paths to follow by scrolling
beyond the boundaries of the screen or jumping to new locations in the
text, movements that exemplify the interactive nature of all reading.
Every reading is different, a reflection of the reader. As writers, students
get to insert and delete words, moving blocks of text and changing the
text's format with instant ease. The machine mediates their decisions as
no paper can, making their words behave more systematically and
strengthening their sense of control over written language.

Looking back, I can see now that what once seemed like diverging interests—literacy and media culture, literature and film, composition and computers—are in fact related. As the profession and the world at large evolve, these disparate directions are converging at all levels. Technologically, computers are being linked increasingly to other media. Students can now link their laptops to printers, faxes, scanners, cameras, CDs, MP3s, DVDs, and the ubiquitous Internet. Textually, this means that the boundaries among different forms of communication are disappearing as our conception of a document takes in more sensory experience and the Web weaves words, graphics, sound bites, and full-motion video into one continuous text. This trend is reflected on the corporate level, as publishers merge with cable companies, television networks, and film studios into multimedia conglomerates. It also echoes through the corridors of academia, informing the research in cognition and multiple intelligences that validates variations in learning styles.

What all this means for the teaching of English, especially at two-year colleges, is that the curriculum can and should expand to keep pace with what we know about learning and our changing culture. As the margins widen into the mainstream, as our nontraditional students become the norm, the most promising paths to literacy are not likely to be through the straits of Hirsch's print-based literacy, but through an inclusive lexicon amplified by the multisensory, multicultural, multimedia character of today's electronic texts. The textbooks for this new curriculum are now being written. My own contribution, *The Writer's Eye*, includes videos, commercials, radio broadcasts, Web sites, and other modern media as texts to be read and composed alongside more traditional academic essays. Our conception of literacy is still expanding, like the branching cactus on my windowsill, nurtured in the open environment of the two-year college.

# Works Cited

Costanzo, W. V. 1984. *Double Exposure: Composing through Writing and Film*. Portsmouth: Boynton.

———. 1989. *The Electronic Text: Learning to Write, Read, and Reason with Computers*. Englewood Cliffs: Educational Technology.

———. 1993. *Literature Tutor*. Software available from the author.

———. 1992. *Reading the Movies: Twelve Great Films on Video and How to Teach Them*. Urbana: NCTE.

———. 2004. *Great Films and How to Teach Them*. Urbana: NCTE.

———. 2005. *The Writer's Eye*. New York: McGraw.

Hirsch, E. D. 1987. *Cultural Literacy: What Every American Needs to Know*. Boston: Houghton.

# 7

## Curriculum Innovation:
## Pursuing Technology in Teaching Composition

### Dee Brock

## Introduction

El Centro College opened in Dallas, Texas, in 1966, the first college in
the Dallas County Community College District (DCCCD). Dallas is a
conservative city today, but thirty years ago, it was often called "ultra
conservative" in almost every respect. Under the inspired leadership of
a dedicated group of civic leaders, however, Dallas passed a sizable bond
issue and the necessary taxing structure to create a multicampus community college system. While two-year colleges had been around for
decades, the community college concept was still relatively new, and the
District's blueprint called for what was then cutting-edge architecture in
the buildings and cutting-edge innovation in the curriculum, learning
tools, and student services. To lead this ambitious enterprise, the district
board selected as chancellor Dr. Bill J. Priest, a recognized leader of the
community college movement, from Sacramento, California.

El Centro College was and continues to be housed in an old, but
beautifully remodeled, department store building in downtown Dallas.
Though the campus has been expanded to take in the entire city block,
it has always retained its original pioneering spirit. *Brown* v. *Brown*
notwithstanding, El Centro was the first integrated educational institution in Dallas. And despite dire predictions of racial discord and other
social ills from those who still clung to the past, the college faculty, staff,
and student body were from the onset exhilaratingly harmonious and
productive.

The first years of the District's history were the "good old days" in
many ways. The faculty and staff were enthusiastic and talented. Student enrollment exceeded initial expectations in numbers, diversity, and
commitment, and continued to grow for over a decade. Within six years,

three more DCCCD colleges had been built, and three more were in various stages of planning. Most importantly, innovation was not only encouraged and appreciated, but there was also sufficient money to support experimentation by those who made a good case for it.

## The Seeds of Innovation

I began teaching English as a member of the inaugural faculty at El Centro College in 1966. There, I had the opportunity to teach an array of courses, from remedial reading and writing to advanced classes in composition and literature. The English faculty worked under the creative leadership of Dr. Dorothy Rushing, the first chair of the department, who encouraged and supported her staff to practice behaviors then unusual in the Texas college scene: Put student learning first; teach students at their own levels and bring them forward at their own pace; value ideas above penmanship and punctuation; and more.

Dr. R. also valued ideas above mere traditional method. If you could think up a way to make student learning more effective or more fun, Dr. R. would support those efforts. Our classrooms sported costumes, dramas, slide shows, dancing, commercially produced and student-produced film and video without stinting. Some of us set up special labs and tutorials, sponsored contests and games, required journals, evaluated papers via audiotape, and team taught. Each of us borrowed without shame the successful practices of colleagues and discarded without mercy the innovations that did not work.

From the beginning, the District actively pursued technologies that could be used to improve instruction that would be effective with the vast range of abilities and many nontraditional students. Though these innovations seem low-tech today, in the late 1960s they were not just high-tech, they were almost esoteric. Computers were not used by most colleges even for business/administrative purposes in 1967 or 1968 when DCCCD recruited and paid for a group of us to participate in a special training program in using the computer for instruction. By understanding the potential of computers, we learned the basics of self-paced learning and branching. We also learned how powerful the computer could be for instructional purposes and, conversely, how easily the computer could be used for boring, repetitive exercises, rather than for intellectually stimulating programs. Back on campus, I used my newly acquired skill to write a number of programmed learning sequences that proved to be successful with students, though lack of easy access to computers at that time made their use unwieldy.

Between 1969 and 1972, several of us faculty garnered the necessary support from the college administration to develop an interdisciplinary two-year program we called the "Mini-College." One purpose was to establish a college within the college, a community of interests to help our students develop a stronger sense of place and form closer relationships with other students—in other words, to simulate some of the benefits of a residential college for the strictly commuting enrollees. A second purpose was to authenticate the interconnections among disciplines. Each involved faculty member—from all of the departments represented in the Mini-College—was also committed to demonstrating that writing well was a necessary skill across disciplines and careers. Students in the program enrolled in at least three common classes a semester, chosen from English, history, philosophy, government, and humanities curricula. They met in small seminar sessions and study groups for single disciplines, as well as cross-disciplinary ones, and in larger gatherings as well.

A key feature of the plan was a weekly meeting of the entire community (usually between 80 and 100 students). These sessions were lively and engaging, even though the group was large. To foster student participation, as well as to improve faculty's insight into the students' collective and individual understandings of the concepts of the day, the District granted my request to purchase an expensive electronic response system for each seat in the lecture hall. This experiment in high-tech support put a control panel in the front of the room through which teachers could see immediate results of polls of students' opinions and questions about their understanding of content and concepts. Actually, we could receive responses from any multiple choice questions. Unfortunately, before I became fully adept at using the system, a new administrative assignment took me away from the Mini-College.

## Television for Instruction

As special assistant to the chancellor, I played a key role in an innovation that had a most significant effect on the profession of teaching English in the two-year college and on my future career: using television to deliver instruction to students away from the campus. Along with others within DCCCD, I was often on a soapbox about using television for college courses. (At the time, *television* meant broadcast television to us.) It seemed clear that other major sectors of society were teaching people through television—who to vote for, what kind of toothpaste to buy, etc.— and we believed that education in Dallas should have its share of this ubiquitous medium that held young and old alike in thrall for many hours every day. And, after all, a few community college leaders were already using television or planning to do so.

Eventually, the administration took up the challenge. Around 1970, the District sent me to study Chicago City College's "College of the Air."

My assignment was to write a report and make recommendations for DCCCD action. I was impressed with the instructional design of the courses and the numbers of students who enrolled. At the same time, I believed that without exorbitant increases in costs, DCCCD could produce programs that were far more engaging and imaginative than the lecture format used in Chicago. Thus, I recommended that the District undertake development of college courses delivered via television because it was a wonderful medium for expanding and enhancing our service to the growing population of Dallas County. I also proposed that we proceed on the idea that education/instruction should be the best programming possible—not the "step child" of the industry.

Accepting these recommendations, the District began exploration of options about where courses would be produced and how they would be aired. Several universities (such as Arizona, Idaho, Nebraska, New York, and Wisconsin, among others) held public television licenses and had production facilities, and DCCCD's friendly rival Coast Community College District in Orange County, California, had opted to create its own station and production house. Because a second educational television channel was available in the Dallas/Fort Worth region, DCCCD gave serious consideration to this possibility. On the pro side were the advantages of controlling both the studio and the airtime schedules. On the down side were the major investments in time and money to acquire the license and plan and build the facility, and the realization that owning and operating an educational television station would require a considerable operational staff and ongoing expenditure. It seemed possible— if not likely—that even if the District's venture into television courses were extremely successful, it might not warrant such an enterprise.

In 1972, while pondering these issues, DCCCD produced its first college credit television course: American Government. The planners selected this course because of its unique importance to higher education in Texas. All graduates of all Texas colleges and universities had to include this course on their transcripts. Further, the particular Texas brand of that subject, which included a unit on Texas government, was a prerequisite for teaching any subject in any state-supported school. Thus, enrollment was always high and always included students who had already earned one or more college degrees and wished to enroll in that course only. Clearly, if there were to be an audience for a college course delivered via television, American Government was the most likely candidate.

The television programs in this first course, which aired on KERA-TV, the local community-licensed PBS station, did not exemplify the high production values we had hoped for, but the instructors and the print materials presented excellent instruction. Most importantly for this new initiative, with almost no promotion, 399 students enrolled the first semester. The percentage of successful completions was very high, and surveys indicated student satisfaction with the experience. The second semester, enrollments increased significantly, and the student successes and satisfaction remained steady. The District expectations were that most enrollees would take the course by television because they could not get into an on-campus section. But overwhelmingly, the students identified other reasons for their choices. Clearly, there was a whole new cadre of students currently unserved by campus classrooms.

In short order, the District began collaborating with Miami-Dade Community College (FL), another innovator in using television to deliver college courses, to tailor its environmental course to DCCCD needs. Soon thereafter, we set our own agenda for the production of a series of new television courses, all featuring the higher production values we desired. Among the first of these new productions, developed in 1974, were a redo of American Government and a new freshman English course. Tarrant County Junior College (TCJC) in Fort Worth came on-board as a partner for these courses. For a contribution to the costs of design and production, TCJC had members of its faculty on the advisory committees and free use of the courses when they aired.

During this period, the partners decided to produce the courses and to continue to broadcast them through KERA-TV. They also agreed to postpone any plans to build a studio and/or to license and activate their own educational broadcast channel. Instead, DCCCD established the Instructional Television (ITV) Center to handle design and production of courses, as well as their administration throughout the District.

## Writing for a Reason

When I was invited to join the ITV Center staff and create the freshman English course, I hoped to develop a literature course and fantasized talking about Greek drama at the Parthenon and Shakespeare plays at Stratford-on-Avon. Composition, however, was a first-semester requirement at DCCCD and, unsurprisingly, the District's choice for the first English course. Though I was sure literature could be presented beautifully and effectively via television, I was less sure that composition could be taught as effectively to students at a distance from their teachers as it could be in face-to-face contact. (Through the years, I frequently found that faculty could often support the use of television in disciplines other than their own, but believed the teacher's presence was required in their own fields.) When Travis Lynn, the first director of the ITV Center, assured me that the ITV Center would invest in the necessary research to determine if the course were effective for students and would shelve the course should it prove unsatisfactory, I began to overcome my concern. When he also committed to invest in changes to make the course better when research indicated the need, the offer became irresistible.

The result was Writing for a Reason (WFR), a college credit composition course. During the period of design and production, I more than once complained that I had to do everything. "Doing everything," in this case, entailed instructional design; writing the scripts; writing the books (student workbook, faculty/administrator's guide, anthology); choosing a handbook; appearing as on-camera "host/teacher"; choosing, recruiting, and working with other actors and interviewees; collecting props; producing segments; writing tests; training the teachers who worked with students; making presentations to the English faculties at DCCCD and TCJC; and working with an advisory council.

Luckily, I had friends—experts in teaching or in television production—who offered pertinent input and generous, loving support. In addition, an excellent faculty advisory committee composed of experienced composition teachers from DCCCD and TCJC evaluated and critiqued design and course elements. The two districts were pleased with the results, and we went into the schedule and on the air in fall 1974.

The goals and content of the course were more classic than revolutionary, as noted in the introduction to students in the study guide:

> The main goal of WRITING FOR A REASON is that you learn to write so effectively that you can fulfill your reasons for writing in college and elsewhere. Consequently, this course will cover basic writing skills, such as choosing and shaping a thesis; planning a composition; composing unified, complete, orderly, and coherent sentences, paragraphs, and essays. Because good writing begins with good thinking, this course will prepare you to think more logically and critically. Because language is the basic medium with which you write, this course will also cover the high points about the way language functions historically, socially, and psychologically. Although grammar and mechanics will not be a part of the course outline, you will receive individual advice about improving your own use of them if you need such help.

Though the goals and content were fairly standard, the nontraditional delivery of the course by necessity changed almost everything. Teachers were still key, but their roles were different. The course required books, but their purposes and uses were different. Students still had to understand concepts and apply them in written papers, but the different environment required different learning and teaching techniques, different support systems, and new communication loops.

In Writing for a Reason, each student, for all practical purposes, took the course alone. Instead of students coming to campus for classroom sessions, television programs were delivered to the homes of the students, each of whom was likely to be watching the programs alone. Though the student could talk to the teacher of record by telephone or by coming to campus, the opportunities that classrooms offer for spur-of-the-moment comments and immediate feedback were missing.

As a consequence, the student study guide became the linchpin of the television course. It integrated all of the course elements for the students—the television programs, the handbook, the anthology, and, of course, the teacher of record. The guide was written in a personal style, as if it were addressed to a single student, and it provided a step-by-step approach to succeeding in the course. In the introductory section, it laid out the course organization, materials, and goals, as well as an effective study plan for this television course. In the body, it set forth specific objectives; helped students identify main points in the television programs and in the readings; and included a multitude of other elements to reinforce concepts presented in the other course materials, such as key terms, study exercises, self-tests with keys. It also included new material germane to the lesson objectives, such as a bibliography and different approaches to the concepts, and readings. The study guide also assigned mail-in essays and offered both a plan of action and tips for success, followed by sample essays of the same type required.

Obviously, the faculty role for a television course was very different from that of a classroom teacher. Like all teachers, the faculty would be responsible for communicating with their students, but in this case, that communication would be almost entirely by phone and mail. Students were required to come to campus for only four meetings—an orientation, during which they would meet their teachers, and three tests. Teachers, however, did not conduct the tests. Instead, students came to a campus test center at times convenient to their personal schedules within a three-day period. Students were invited, but not required, to attend three on-site discussion sessions as well. Though many faculty wanted to require more face-to-face meetings, the decision for DCCCD was that this course was developed to provide a new approach to teaching composition and a new way to reach students at a distance, not merely to serve as a supplement to classroom instruction. Consequently, the number was not increased.

To help faculty understand and excel in their new roles, the course provided both a guidebook and training seminars for those who would be teachers of record. Communication was the key issue. Among other suggestions and directions, the *Telecourse Procedures Notebook*, a guide for faculty and administrators, identified many different communication techniques and provided samples of most of those that make the communication connection through the written word, such as a welcoming letter (suggested) and a syllabus (required).

The television programs and the student guide were designed to be used for more than one semester, and we always assumed that we would market the course and individual programs to many different colleges. Though I was responsible for determining the assignments for DCCCD, other colleges could change those requirements if they wished. As a result of these parameters, no assignments were made via the television programs. Rather, all were made in the student guide, which printed no due dates. Thus, the syllabus—complete with dates for papers, test schedules, the semester broadcast schedule, and any changes to the plan laid out in the student guide—was critical.

The student assignments were fairly traditional and rigorous. Students were required to write eleven mail-in papers, in addition to three examinations, all including essays, during the term. Though comments about their writing are always important for students, for students at a distance, prompt, personalized, and pithy feedback on their writing is even more crucial than it is for others. When teachers see their students regularly several hours a week, they can deal with some problems in class, and students can easily ask questions and get answers. Television students must be dealt with individually. At that time, WFR teachers returned comments to students primarily via the mail; thus, it was especially important that papers be turned around quickly. (Today, of course, many teachers and students use e-mail for prompt communication.)

Another critical purpose of the faculty notebook and seminars was to develop a common way for judging the papers. Up to that point, there was little, if any, guidance about how to evaluate papers for English faculties at DCCCD and TCJC (a condition I believe was true in most colleges). Teachers were free to interpret the textbooks as they wished and to set the standards for their students as they wished. In WFR sections, however, the students would be receiving their primary instruction from the course materials, not from their instructor of record.

The faculty agreed that it would be unfair and counterproductive if they graded papers according to principles other than those set forth in the television course. Each writing assignment contained clear instructions and sample papers with marginal notes pointing out the way the authors handled the requirements. Following the samples was a checklist for students to use to evaluate their own work before submitting it. The Faculty Guide included a corresponding checklist for faculty to use in evaluating student papers and a suggested "mathematical breakdown" on elements such as content, overall organization, paragraph development, and so on. Through serious and lively discussions before and during the semester, WFR faculty managed to come to consensus about how the instructors would fulfill their roles as teachers and as evaluators.

To facilitate communication, we mandated a special two-part carbon paper designed by TCJC faculty to be used by students for their essays. Students mailed their essays with the two-part form intact; teachers made their comments on the form and returned one part to students. Thus, both the teacher and the student could have on hand a copy of the essay and the comments when they talked about the paper on the phone. The mail-in address, lacking only the name of the teacher, was printed on the back of each carbon sheet so that students could fold and mail their papers without envelopes.

We all believed that personal communication with the students was important. Some of us sent students audiotapes containing our comments about their papers, in the belief that the spoken word, even with hesitations, stutters, and mistakes, added a valuable human note for the student away from the campus. In addition, we developed a number of audiotapes and accompanying worksheets for students needing remediation or reinforcement of basic course concepts.

Attempting to incorporate the latest research in learning theory, we praised every aspect of the papers that we could. When pointing out flaws, we made suggestions for improvement, rather than merely pointing out what was wrong. We avoided using abbreviations only, even for mechanical problems. Instead, we might write a brief explanation or send along a study sheet with examples or an audiotape with a worksheet. To facilitate rapid return of student papers, we prepared in advance explanations of many of the most common problems and ways to correct them, but we consistently referenced these standard explanations to each individual's work. To further personalize our comments, we referred to the student by name at least once on each paper, signed our own names to our responses, and tried to write at least one nonjudgmental comment responding simply to the student's voice or message.

Over eight hundred students enrolled in DCCCD sections and several hundred more enrolled in TCJC sections the first semester the course was offered (fall 1974). The demographics for WFR, as well as the other courses offered via television during my tenure at the ITV Center, revealed similar characteristics to those for the first American Government television course. Compared to on-campus students, television students were older; more of them were women; fewer of them were working toward a degree; more of them had full-time jobs outside their homes. (A significant number were mothers of small children who had full-time jobs inside their homes.) The three most important reasons for taking the course via television were avoiding traditional classes, the convenience of not having to drive to campus (public transportation was not an option in much of Dallas County), and the ability to work around job and family responsibilities. About one-third of the students indicated that they would not have taken the course had it not been offered on television.

The success of WFR and other new college credit television courses prompted increased production by community colleges and many new partnerships among these producers. In addition, the ability of the courses to attract unserved populations and to meet students' learning needs motivated other colleges—two-year and four-year institutions—to approach DCCCD and other producers for permission to offer such courses to their communities. As a result, WFR was soon in use by many other colleges and universities.

## Testing the Efficacy of WFR

Within the first two years, student surveys, completion rates, and student grades each semester convinced us that WFR was working, but we still needed to prove it. Thus in 1976, we developed a pre- and post-course essay to evaluate Writing for a Reason. All students enrolled in WFR were included in the study. Additionally, other students enrolled in traditional daytime and evening classes were included, which allowed us to compare both on-campus and television students—those taught by different teachers and those taught by the same teacher, as well as daytime, evening, and television students. Not every teacher of record read the essays; instead we organized a group of excellent composition teachers and read the papers in a group setting after achieving consensus about evaluation standards.

The results were strikingly positive. Overall, there was a significant improvement across the board in student papers during the course of the semester. Students enrolled in the television course actually performed better than those on campus. The immediate reaction of the Director of the ITV Center was that this last fact should not be publicized. First, he believed it would cause unnecessary unease in the on-campus faculty at a time when television courses were new. Second, we didn't really know how to explain this difference (which was statistically significant, but not extraordinary). Perhaps it was that television students were older, more focused, more dedicated to their work.

Other parts of the research included student and faculty surveys about most useful and least useful elements, needed and suggested changes, and overall satisfaction with the course and the way it did (or did not) help them accomplish the stated goals. Student surveys were included as part of the final examination, and the responses were pleasingly positive.

We also attempted to reach by mail and by phone those who did not complete the term—both those who officially dropped out and those who simply quit participating. The response rate for this element of the evaluation was quite low; apparently students who did not want to finish the course did not want to answer questions about it either. Most of those who did respond, however, indicated that they dropped out for personal reasons—new jobs, new babies, marital difficulties, illnesses—rather than because of the course itself. Still, some found the course too difficult or too time-consuming; some also discovered they were not self-directed enough to work as independently as the course required.

## The Professional Benefits

Over time, many teachers at DCCCD and across the country told me that their experiences with Writing for a Reason had given them new perspectives about communicating with students and teaching composition. Faculty often commented that they used the evaluation guides in the faculty notebook for other classes. Many noted how much more objective their evaluations of papers were when they knew the authors only through their writing. While this insight did not keep them from wanting to know all of their students better, it did shed new light on the way they graded papers. Several also expressed their surprise in learning how much they depended on the force of their own personalities in their teaching and their relationships with students. As teachers of WFR, their personal charm and wisdom were known primarily through their writing. It was, thus, important that they not only preach, but also practice, good writing skills.

Student surveys also gave teachers insights they could apply to on-campus classes. For example, students always placed the organization of WFR and the fact that the entire course plan was laid out from the first of the term among the characteristics they liked best. Not surprisingly, students disliked delays in receiving the teacher's comments on their papers.

Not all teachers who tried WFR liked being the teacher of record. For some, the classroom experience was their reason for teaching. Evaluating papers and helping students revise them was the price they were willing to pay for doing what they liked best—face-to-face interaction with students. Further, not all of them believed that students could learn to improve their writing skills sufficiently from the television course, despite our research and without any comparable studies of their own. In fact, the English faculty at some community colleges in California organized to remove WFR from their colleges' television curriculum.

Faculty for WFR and television courses in general often worried that television courses would take jobs away from full-time faculty. Many colleges did staff television courses with part-timers, though more often they staffed them as overload classes for full-time faculty. As a rule, WFR sections included about the same number of students as on-campus composition classes at each institution. (That fact was not necessarily true of courses in other disciplines, where the time commitment for evaluating student work was significantly less.) Actually, I personally have never known of a faculty position lost because of television.

Not all teachers who tried teaching WFR were good at it. Some could not keep up with the grading and the other communication requirements. Some just could not get the hang of communicating with students at a distance. On the other hand, many taught the course for years, and when WFR was replaced, they continued to teach composition through the newer DCCCD composition television courses.

## Summing Up WFR

Overall, WFR was successful beyond our expectations. The most important reason, of course, was that it worked—students really learned. Second, the course had staying power. It served hundreds of students in DCCCD each semester it was used, and it was used every semester for ten years. Like other television courses, it also proved very versatile. It was used at home, at work, in libraries, and in other community centers through a variety of delivery systems. Classroom teachers used individual programs as supplementary information and as library assignments.

Additionally, we were able to implement a nationwide marketing plan, and the course was licensed and used by many hundreds of colleges and universities across the country for many years. As Dr. Priest noted, we were thus able to share our costs, as well as our expertise, with our colleagues. Not insignificantly, this course, along with other television courses, made college instruction accessible to millions of students who might otherwise have had to delay or abandon their hopes for higher education.

In fall 1984, DCCCD replaced Writing for a Reason with The Write Course, and in fall 1995, the District replaced that course with The Writer's Exchange. Both of these newer courses have been used or are being used by hundreds of colleges as well. They both reflect the change in the profession from viewing writing as a solitary task to focusing on collaboration as a primary skill in composition. The student success rate for these newer courses demonstrates that even students physically alone can learn the skills and techniques of collaborative writing. They can then put these into effect through the skillful use of the written or spoken word via paper, telephone, computer, and in-person meetings as guided by the course materials. At the same time, the skills featured in WFR are still valid and in vogue. At least, my colleagues at the DCCCD Le Croy Center for Telecommunications, the fabulous replacement for the old ITV Center, tell me that some programs from WFR are still used via cable, closed circuit, and VCR even today.

## Going National

In 1975, the second year WFR was on the air, I accepted the position of Director of Information and Marketing for the ITV Center.

In 1980, I left DCCCD to join the Public Broadcasting Service (PBS) to develop the PBS Adult Learning Service (ALS), the first nationally coordinated service delivering college-credit television courses to local colleges and universities for broadcast via their local PBS stations. WFR did not go with me to PBS; however, four Dallas courses were in our first ALS lineup at PBS. Since then ALS has offered most new Dallas television courses, including new composition courses, and Dallas productions remain ALS's most well-used offerings. This PBS service still regularly provides television courses that serve hundreds of thousands of students a year through some 2,000 local colleges and universities.

Later, we developed the PBS Adult Learning Satellite Service (ALSS), the first and largest direct satellite service to colleges and universities. Still growing, ALSS provides teleconferences, short courses, courses for cable and VCR, previews for broadcast courses, and other kinds of educational programming and information. Before I left PBS, we had also expanded the adult learning opportunities to include a special programming service for businesses and another for K–12 teachers.

During the 1980s, PBS and hundreds of colleges/ universities, businesses, and other sectors were actively using or exploring the educational and instructional uses of many technologies—cable, fiber optics, closed circuit interactive television, T-1 lines, computer-based instruction delivered via several media, and more. The 1990s saw both the exploration and the use of new technologies for education accelerate wildly. In truth, the opportunities for students worldwide to learn on every level via technology and at a distance from the source of the instruction continue to proliferate.

Based on past experiences, I am certain that two-year colleges with their innovative faculties and their diverse student populations will continue to be on the cutting edge of major innovations in teaching English.

## Note

For further information about the DCCCD college-credit television courses noted here, their books and other ancillary materials, the full catalog of television courses produced by DCCCD, or the full range of instructional technologies currently in use or under development by the Le Croy Telecommunication Center, contact the Director of Marketing, Jan Le Croy Center for Telecommunications, 12800 Abrams Road, Dallas, TX 75243.

For further information about PBS educational services and/or programming, contact Director of Marketing, PBS Education, Public Broadcasting Service, 1320 Braddock Place, Alexandria, VA 22314.

# 8

## Coming of Age in ESL:
## Memoirs of a Reluctant Pioneer

### Alan Meyers

## Introduction

The City Colleges of Chicago (CCC) were long past the formative stages when I joined the faculty in 1968. The first junior college appeared there in the late 1920s, with most of the seven other colleges added after World War II. All but two colleges rented or were granted space in city high schools, with the exception of Loop College downtown and Wright College, where I began my career. Wilbur Wright Junior College occupied a converted junior high school building on the northwest side of the city and was affectionately known as UCLA (the University of Chicago Located on Austin Avenue). The reference to the University of Chicago was not accidental, for the junior college system modeled itself on the liberal arts curriculum of the Hyde Park matriarch. The shift from junior to community college had occurred just prior to my arrival, when in 1966 the colleges severed connections with the Chicago Public School System and appointed Oscar Shabat as the first chancellor.

## Was It Like This at Kitty Hawk?

Wright was somewhat typical of the non-inner-city campuses in CCC at the time. The student body comprised blue-collar, first- and second-generation ethnic Americans, most of whom were Italian, Polish, or Irish, with only a smattering of blacks and immigrants. The faculty were past middle-age, overwhelmingly white, and settled (some might argue fossilized) in their ways. But the City Colleges' newly gained independence from the Board of Education had led to rapid expansion of programs, necessitating the hiring of many new faculty. Wright employed sixteen young instructors in English over a two-year period (I was twenty-three when I started), swelling the English department to forty-eight, and lowering the average age of the entire faculty to fifty-six! The department offered English 101 and 102, English 100, various reading courses, thirty-eight sections of literature, and two or three sections of English as a Second Language (ESL) for the few Middle Eastern and Latin American students on campus.

My fresh-out-of-graduate-school colleagues and I of course fancied ourselves revolutionaries, or at least reformers. Antiwar and left-leaning, we had read the required texts by John Holt, Paul Goodman, David Herndon, Jonathan Kozol, Neil Postman and Charles Weingartner, Ken Macrorie, et al., and thus struggled to empower our students, end poverty, racism, sexism, and bring greater progress through chemistry. Although our students were disinclined to join us in storming the ramparts, my young colleagues and I spent countless hours in our office cubicles, in bars, and in each other's apartments discussing educational philosophy and methodology, sharing materials, and arguing politics.

I taught virtually every course in the department over the next eight years, experimented with a variety of techniques and fads, and team-taught in an interdisciplinary program that gave rise to my first textbook, a speech communications book written collaboratively with Karen Carlson from the speech department. I loved language, grammar, and style, but knew virtually nothing about the ways of language acquisition of immigrants and refugees. I taught an occasional ESL course, but with little distinction or success.

All that changed in 1976, when through attrition and structural modifications, I found myself thirtieth in seniority in a department of twenty-nine, suddenly transferred to the communications department (English, speech, and ESL) of Harry S Truman College. The name was new, replacing Amundson-Mayfair College, and so was the campus, housed in two Chicago public school buildings located in the Uptown neighborhood, a traditional debarkation point for new arrivals to the country and the city. Thus I encountered a new breed of students, few of whom were native speakers of the language.

## Saigon Fall, Right into Truman's Lap

Of necessity, Truman's English as a Second Language classes grew rapidly in scope and breadth. The communications department offered three levels of ESL, each of which comprised three courses (English, reading, speech) for a total of nine hours of credit. Many of my new colleagues had been teaching within the program for a decade, but I was immediately daunted by the students.

These non-English-dominant folk came from more than 100 countries, spoke over 70 different languages, and presented a multitude of challenges. Take, for example, the simple matter of pronouncing (and identifying students by) their names. Upon entering an ESL class at Truman just after the fall of Saigon, I discovered twenty or so appellations like *Xuan Cao Nguyen* on the class roster. Always resourceful, I decided to have the group members introduce themselves so I could correlate sound with orthography.

The first student rose, bowed, and announced: "My name *Chong Chong*, and I from Vietnam."

The next student rose, bowed, and announced, "My name *Chong Chong*, and I from Vietnam." There were twenty *Chong Chongs* in the class.

Names from virtually every land presented challenges. All the Koreans were Parks, Lees, or Kims, and their first (or was it last?) names gave no hint of gender. How could I distinguish an Iraqi from an Iranian? (And was that guy Hussein Mohammed or Mohammed Hussein?) What about Maria Lopez Gonzalez? Did I call her Ms. Lopez or Ms. Gonzalez? How could I pronounce that Thai student's eighteen-syllable name? The parade of proper nouns marched through my classes in never-ending variety. The Patels, Singhs, and Shaikhs. The Adeniyis and Nwosus. The Krpos, Radus, and Alijagics. The Raghunanans and Mansoors. Nonetheless, I soon came to admire the intelligence, industriousness, and courage of these individuals, who believed in the American dream and the value of education. I read extensively about their histories and cultures and consulted my atlas on a regular basis.

My ignorance of their lives and histories was exceeded only by my newfound ignorance of English grammar, a subject I had always loved. The language was far more complex than I had realized, and my students forced me to examine its complexity daily. For example, the subject–verb in questions and negatives had a number of unexpected permutations, some requiring simple inversions, others the addition of a helping verb. Moreover, verb tenses in complex sentences related to each other oddly. Why, for instance, was it correct to say, "I *will transfer* to the University of Illinois after I finish my courses at Truman" but not, as my students said, "*after I will finish*"? And why did some verbs take gerund objects, some infinitives, and some either: "He enjoys swimming," "He wants to swim" and "He loves swimming/to swim." (And what exactly is the difference between "I stopped smoking" and "I stopped to smoke"?)

The noun determiner system, so intuitive to native speakers, surprised me more. Who had ever thought that nouns could be countable or uncountable? And who knew what governed the choices among *a/an, the*, or no article? I fretted out my own rules, which, regrettably, still cannot account for every idiomatic construction. Why do the British say "going to hospital," while Americans say "going to *the* hospital"? (And why should the

British construction sound odd when we say "going to school or work"?) Why do we say *the* Mississippi River but not *the* Lake Michigan?

And idioms were countless and inexplicable. (Why do "burn up" and "burn down?" mean the same? And why do we "fix" breakfast when it isn't broken?) My students despaired at learning all the simple verb–preposition combinations that express a myriad of idiomatic meanings: *get up, get down, get off, get on, get in, get out, get over, get away with, get on with, get around, get back, get at,* and so on.

## It's a Material Question

In my years at Wright, I had routinely invented materials, sometimes eschewing textbooks completely, but at Truman I depended heavily on books. Like everyone in the communications department, I used the *American English* series and texts by Robert J. Dixon. Unschooled in foreign language instruction, I sought the help of colleagues, who taught me methodology: demonstrate, drill, explain if necessary, then move to production of the grammatical structure in a meaningful context. The materials and procedures worked, but not ideally. The books were too old, too mechanical, and too devoid of explanations for students who wished to study at home. They wanted to know when to use a structure, what message it conveyed, and how it related to cognate structures (if they existed) in their languages. Above all, they needed guided instruction in writing, for their uncontrolled expression seemed a tower of Babel assembled by Rube Goldberg.

The recurring problems among people from the same language group began to fascinate me: the missing subjects before verbs among the Spanish speaking (and, of course, the comma-spliced and run-on sentences), the lack of distinction between nouns, verbs, and adjectives among the Vietnamese, Koreans, and Chinese, the absence of past-tense forms for *can, will,* and *be* among the Filipinos, the insertion of the helping verb *be* in virtually all constructions among the East Indians. I became a language detective, asking students how such structures operated in their native tongues. Not surprisingly, I learned that many Asian languages lack part-of-speech inflections; that Spanish verb inflections contain the subject (and, of course, that commas join independent clauses); that Tagalog and other Filipino languages do not inflect the verb *to be* for tense or agreement (the inflection falls on the verb complement); that Hindi employs the helping verb *to be* and *-ing* constructions in infinite variety; and that many languages do not distinguish between specific and nonspecific nouns. My detective work continues to this day, for the student body continues to change. The maxim at Truman is that six months to a year after a war, famine, revolution, or campaign of persecution, new immigrants or refugees will be sitting in our ESL classrooms. We've welcomed Hmong, Vietnamese, Nigerians, Thais, Laotians, Cambodians, Haitians, Dominicans, Mexicans, Puerto Ricans, Assyrians, Ethiopians (later Eritreans), Palestinians, Iraqis, Iranians, Poles, Romanians, Bangladeshis, Chinese, Guatemalans, Salvadorians, Cubans, Bosnians, and scores of other nationalities.

Perhaps most significantly in those first years at Truman, I found that ESL teaching was not limited to the ESL classes. My "remedial" English 100 classes were filled with "native" students whose primary language was not English, yet the available remedial/developmental texts ignored such first-language interference issues. I began to intuit the rules for the chapters on articles, prepositions, and verb constructions in my second textbook, *Writing with Confidence*, which contributed largely to its success. My colleague Ethel Tiersky and I later cowrote a four-book series called *Toward American English*. Our goals were to provide a meaningful (and often humorous) context in which to place grammatical structures; and to integrate speaking, listening, pronunciation, reading, and writing within that context.

Prior to writing the series, Ethel and I surveyed the field, and our research revealed the chaotic state of ESL delivery systems throughout the country. Instruction ranged from free courses in church basements stressing survivor-skill English, to credit programs in academic English in community and four-year colleges, to supplemental course work for international students in graduate school. The wildly disparate responses to our manuscript from such disparate reviewers led to constant revisions and delays, so our two-year project stretched into three.

Truman's ESL program grew exponentially during the late 1970s and 1980s. Unprecedented numbers of immigrants and refugees poured into Uptown and surrounding communities. As the members of the communications department became more sophisticated about the problems of language acquisition and proficiency, we expanded our offerings, adding first one and then two writing courses to precede English 101. We learned that learning to write in a second language is slow, hard work.

# The Russians Are Coming, the Russians Are Coming!

Nothing could have prepared the communications department faculty for the arrival of refugees from the western provinces of the Soviet Union in 1977. The first group of thirty, most of whom were women, surfaced in the summer when I taught a pilot ESL class. The real challenge wasn't their language learning; it was their behavior.

They talked! Incessantly! (I quickly acquired the most important word in the Russian language: *ticha*.) And they cheated in ways I hadn't seen since grammar school: ponies under test booklets and in purses open on the floor, writing on desktops, hand signals, notes on their forearms, even on their knees. A favorite ploy was to send a student to my desk to distract me with a question while the remainder of the class exchanged words, notes, and whole compositions.

One day near the end of the term, an elderly Russian woman asked me if she and her husband could repeat the course. "Boris, he don't hear so good, and me, mine heart is a problem, so we think maybe you should giving us *D*'s and we take once more your class next semester."

"OK, Ludmila," I agreed. "You and Boris can repeat."

Despite our agreement, Ludmila and Boris appeared for the final examination and occupied their customary seats in the first row. What a good idea, I thought, for I can at least determine where they need improvement. Ten minutes into the test, however, I noticed some odd behavior from Boris, who kept lifting up the corners of his test paper. Curious, I walked over to his desk, picked up the exam, and found a complete list of the irregular verbs written on the desktop in pencil. Old habits die hard.

Thus I added another area of expertise to my repertoire: test proctoring. The class period before each examination, I announced with great ceremony and humor that students would sit in every other seat, no books would be opened, all purses would be closed, desktops and knees would be inspected, and no questions would be asked. "Ah," they observed, "you have rich knowledge!"

While struggling to control the revolutions in my classrooms conducted by those sons and daughters of the Bolsheviks, I also struggled with the language issues they introduced. Russian is so highly inflected that word order plays virtually no role in expressing grammatical relationships. And, of course, the language lacks articles before nouns.

Soon the trickle of Russians turned into a deluge, as nearly a thousand former denizens of Kiev, Lvov, Leningrad, and Moscow doubled the size of our program. Sections in ESL course offerings grew from 50 to 100 and then to almost 250. Truman became *the* ESL community college in Chicago, the largest in the state, and among the largest in the country (Ignarsh 57). The department swelled to 45 as we hired new full-time faculty, some with advanced degrees in linguistics or TESL (Teaching English as a Second Language)—our first specialists in the field.

# Enlist More Troops
# (as Long as We Don't Have to Give Them Benefits)

As the number of classes continued to grow, full-time faculty could no longer handle the load. Meanwhile, state and city revenues for the City Colleges fell while operating expenses rose, especially in the cost of employee health care. The communications department thus resorted to a new, bargain-basement (in cost, not quality) staffing resource—the adjunct. Prior to 1980, an occasional outside lecturer taught a course or two, but over the next decade the occasions became far more frequent. The number of adjunct faculty ballooned to seventy by spring 1990 and threatened to reach ninety by fall. Not surprisingly, our beleaguered department chair announced his resignation in spring 1990 and asked me to stand for election. I declined, then demurred, then finally acquiesced on the condition that the administration provide me with two full-time assistants. The president of the college similarly declined, demurred, and then acquiesced when he realized I left him with no other choice. Ethel Tiersky joined ranks with another colleague, Marine Hoover, as my assistant chairs, and we immediately set to work.

Over the summer, the three of us advertised our openings for adjuncts, interviewed candidates in hope of staffing every TBA class (132 in all) by the first day of the fall semester. We had security open the campus building for us on the Saturday before Labor Day so we could coordinate our phone-calling efforts, and that Sunday Ethel interviewed an applicant in her kitchen. We succeeded in staffing every course, many by instructors with no previous experience in ESL, and brought in a nearby university's TESOL department chair to conduct a two-day orientation, prepared handouts on procedures, and solicited volunteer mentors from among the full-time faculty. Our efforts more or less worked and garnered the communications department a reputation for efficiency and ingenuity throughout the City Colleges, although, of course, I have had to fight to retain my assistant chairs a half dozen times since.

## We Wage the Remedial Wars

An enlightened, professional program does not necessarily engender an enlightened legislature and central administration, especially with the frequent turnover among board members, chancellors, and vice chancellors. Small skirmishes and major warfare have broken out throughout the past decade. The battle lines are normally drawn with an inquiry. "Why," a new downtown general, corporal, or staff sergeant asks, "does the credit program offer remedial courses in ESL?"

"Because ESL isn't remedial; it's foreign language instruction," we reply. "Remedial instruction fills deficits in previous education, and our students don't lack education. In fact, quite the contrary; many were professionals in their native countries. Besides, they're taking calculus, biology, and physical science as well. If it weren't for the presence of the ESL students in those classes, you'd have to cancel half of them and deprive the native-born students."

"Hmm," the officer of the district counters. "We'll have to explore this issue further."

Then follow the memos, meetings, and meanderings through the bureaucracy. An uneasy peace endures for a year or two until the administration changes and the familiar attacks resume. However, like any warrior concerned with postwar environmental cleanup, I've learned to conserve and recycle the detritus—that is, my memoranda. Why compose new arguments when they haven't changed in decades? I've also learned to engage in conflict judiciously, sparring, then retreating, and cutting my losses so as not to lose the war. Nevertheless, the casualties continue to mount. Over the last ten years the three lowest levels of our program have been eliminated, with nearly sixty sections slashed in one semester. The troops in the communications department have diminished to twenty-three full-time faculty and perhaps forty-five adjuncts. My life may have been simplified as a result, though. I even find time to watch a Cubs game these days.

And now, at this writing, I'm fifty-nine, a year older than the average Wright College faculty member in 1968, when I set out to change the world. Somewhere in my attic is a Free Bobby Seale button.

# Works Cited

Carlson, K., and A. Meyers. 1977. *Speaking with Confidence*. Glenview: Scott.

Dixon, R. J. 1956. *Regents English Workbook*. 3 vols. New York: Regents.

Goodman, P. 1960. *Growing Up Absurd*. New York: Random.

Herndon, J. 1968. *The Way It Spozed to Be*. New York: Bantam.

———. 1971. *How to Survive in Your Native Land*. New York: Bantam.

Holt, John. 1964. *How Children Fail*. New York: Dell.

———. 1967. *How Children Learn*. New York: Dell.

Ignarsh, J. M. 1994. "Compelling Numbers: English as a Second Language." In *Relating Curriculum and Transfer*, edited by Arthur M. Cohen. *New Directions for Community Colleges* 86, 49–62. San Francisco: Jossey.

Kozol, J. 1967. *Death at an Early Age*. New York: Bantam.

Macrorie, K. 1970. *Uptaught*. Rochelle Park: Hayden.

———. 1974. *A Vulnerable Teacher*. Rochelle Park: Hayden.

Meyers, A. 1979. *Writing with Confidence*. Glenview: Scott.

Meyers, A., and E. Tiersky. 1984. *Toward American English*. 2 vols. Glenview: Scott.

Nadler, H., et al. 1971. *American English Grammatical Structure*. 3 vols. Chicago: Rand.

Postman, N., and Charles W. 1971. *The Soft Revolution*. New York: Dell.

# 9

## Roger Garrison (1918–1984): Teacher of Teachers

### Mary Sue Koeppel

Picture a gray-bearded, curly-haired man in lumberjack-plaid shirt sitting at a baby grand black piano pounding out Beethoven's "Apassionata," tears streaming down his cheeks, foot stamping on the soft pedal. That was Roger H. Garrison to hundreds and hundreds of community-college faculty. Garrison never explained why he wept as he entertained at the baby grand; we only knew that he was moved and so were we.

Picture a small New England college with red brick buildings surrounding a green, and a tiny sugar-cube art museum building tucked in a corner holding Van Gogh's *Irises* (yes, the original that later sold for millions) and a Picasso or two. Grasp a metaphor. On this tiny campus, community-college faculty were first treated to the historically important National Institute for Teachers of Writing and the National Master Teacher Seminars, both begun by Roger H. Garrison.

For eleven successive summers, beginning in 1973, Garrison organized and directed the National Institute for Community College English Instructors Who Teach Writing (aka The National Institute for Teachers of Writing) at Westbrook College in Portland, Maine.

A professional writer and editor and a longtime two-year-college teacher and administrator, Garrison wrote influential books and articles on community-college teaching and staff development. But to writing instructors, Garrison is best known for his pioneer work in teaching the writing process and one-to-one writing instruction.

"Composition," Garrison said, "is probably the most difficult course to teach of any in a college program." His efforts as writer and teacher aimed at making that difficult course easier for teachers and, most importantly, productive for students. How did Garrison approach that problem?

Follow his thoughts in one of his famous lectures to teachers. Garrison quoted Alfred North Whitehead: "Knowledge, like fish, grows old after three days." You cannot just offer students knowledge; students have to be able to do something with their knowledge. "A merely well-informed man is the world's most useless bore," he said. Garrison believed that the teacher's role is to give students the tools of their discipline so students can act in the discipline. "Using an idea means relating that idea to the stream, that compound of sense perceptions, feelings, hopes, desires, and mental activities of adjusting thought to thought which forms our life," he claimed. Teach students to see relationships, meanings, connections. But what does this mean to the composition teacher?

Garrison believed that all disciplines have several lifelong skills. It is the teacher's job to find these three or four skills, and to teach them superbly, in relationship to larger contexts, so that the students will have mastered the skills for life.

To illustrate his thinking, Garrison often asked professionals to name the three or four skills basic to their professions. Thus when Garrison asked film director John Ford to name the three or four basics, the kernels of a good movie, Ford answered, "The long shot, the midshot, and the close-up." Only after mastering those might a director create a fine film.

So in teaching composition, Garrison believed, the instructor's goal is to find the several skills that students must master and teach those skills completely, superbly. Out of this philosophy grew Garrison's teaching of writing as process and his methodology, the one-to-one instruction.

Garrison isolated the skills he expected the students to master: choosing a workable idea, collecting supporting details, choosing a point of view (audience and purpose), organizing and drafting material, rewriting and rewriting some more, polishing grammar and style. Students developed these skills, often with several one-on-one discussions with the instructor during the writing of each paper. Garrison firmly believed that each one-on-one ought to be short (perhaps only three or so minutes), concentrating on just one or two of the skills good writers must master. Thus a student whose paper reflected several topics had a conference about settling on only one topic (the student's choice, of course), or a student whose paper offered only a scattering of details had a discussion of ways to gather sufficient information. Only after the decisions about topic, supporting details, point of view, and organization were settled did the instructor and student engage in a one-on-one discussion of sentence style or diction. Thus instructor and student conferred about only one important writing matter at a time. Neither instructor nor student was overwhelmed.

Because Garrison had been a professional writer (in Hollywood and for national magazines) before he began teaching writing, he knew how writers work, and so he devised his one-on-one approach, revolutionary in the 1960s and 70s, but taken for granted today. Garrison believed that writers learn to write by writing and a teacher of writing teaches best, not by lecturing about writing, but by being at the student's elbow to guide and help at all stages of the writing process (thus his emphasis on the writing process and his guides for meaningful intervention). Garrison believed that face-to-face intervention was much more valuable to the students than pages of red ink on the students' final papers. It is much to Garrison's credit that both an understanding of process and the practice of conferences (individual or collaborative) are now no longer revolutionary, but commonplace.

Because Garrison was himself a two-year-college instructor, he understood the many problems confronting composition teachers of first-generation college students, especially because so many of them had had little or no formal training in the teaching of writing. Based on their classroom experiences with two-year-college students, most two-year faculty readily embraced Garrison's methods.

From 1973 until his death in 1984, Garrison taught his approach to teaching writing to thousands of community college faculty in both his National Institute for Teachers of Writing and in workshops on many college campuses. After his death, his handpicked colleagues of the National Institute for Teachers of Writing staff—Nancy Roedigger of Tarrant County Junior College, Texas; Mary Sue Koeppel of Florida Community College at Jacksonville; and Robert B. Gentry of Florida Community College at Jacksonville—continued the Institute and maintained Garrison's teaching methodology. By the end of the 80s, the staff moved the summer National Institute for Teachers of Writing to Greenfield, Massachusetts, where the Institute functioned during summers until 1994.

Garrison described his methods in his seminal article "One-to-One: Tutorial Instruction in Freshman Composition" published in *New Directions for Community Colleges* early in 1974. His method was tested and the overwhelmingly positive results reported in the famous *Improvement of Learning in English Project: One-to-One Instructors' Manual* by the Division of Educational Services, Office of Instructional Services of the Los Angeles Community College District in 1982. Jo An McGuire Simmons reported on the Garrison method and its successful use in the Los Angeles Community College District in 1984 in *College Composition and Communication.*

Several contemporary college composition textbooks written by two-year-college teachers develop their materials so that interested instructors can easily employ variations on the Garrison methods of instruction, e.g., Dornan and Dawe's *One to One Resources for Conference Centered Writing*, Koeppel's *Writing Resources for Conferencing and Collaboration* and her *Writing Strategies, Plus Collaboration.*

Garrison's inimitable effect on the community-college world is not limited, however, to his teaching and writing about writing. In the 1960s, he experienced, he often said, a new phenomenon—a community college opening at the rate of almost one a week (for example, fifty opened in 1965 and fifty more in 1966). With grants received from both the United States Steel Foundation and the American Association of Junior Colleges, Garrison spent fourteen months studying these colleges and the needs of the new community college faculty. He published his findings and recommendations in a highly influential book, *Junior College Faculty: Issues and Problems* (1967). One year later, his important *Teaching in a Junior College: A Brief Professional Orientation* was published by the American Association of Junior Colleges.

As he traveled around the country doing his studies of the fast-growing junior colleges, he often witnessed classes taught using traditional methods by faculty members who had little understanding of the special needs of the community college student. And, Garrison said, he also witnessed brilliance in the classroom. Great teachers, according to Garrison, stimulate their students. How? He'd quote William James: "I stir up the animals and wait to see what happens."

To illustrate fine teaching, Garrison was fond of describing an extraordinary history professor he discovered teaching a typical community-college survey history course. Being a great teacher, this man knew he couldn't just lecture; instead, he had to *choose* and *teach exquisitely well* a few important points of each of the centuries he was to cover, and he had to get his adult students involved. It was the 60s, so for a study of political theory, the professor assigned the students to read *The Prince* by Machiavelli; then he broke his class into small groups and gave them one week to devise a plan to bring down the administration of their college using only Machiavelli's theories. Those students of the 60s, themselves in the midst of campus turmoil, Garrison said, would never forget that history lesson. In that classroom, he witnessed his own philosophy of teaching a few ideas superbly.

But even as Garrison discovered great teachers during his travels to the colleges in his study, he realized that little was being done to prepare most instructors for their unique work in the growing community-college system. In response to the need, he decided that if he could get fifty or a hundred community-college teachers together and supply them with basic comforts (good food and drinks, comfortable dorm rooms, and time), they would share ideas and approaches, thereby improving community-college teaching across the nation. Thus originated his famous, and often copied, National Master Teacher Seminars for two-year-college faculty.

These seminars began in Portland, Maine, in 1969, although he had conducted other seminars since 1962 in New York. His Master Teacher Seminar concept, soon picked up by the Great Teachers Movement out of Illinois, was later replicated in many community colleges in the United States and Canada. Garrison's Master Teacher Seminars for community-college teachers were based on his study of the growing community-college system and his own simpler, but profound, premises:

1. Teachers learn best from each other. Well-facilitated shoptalk can be the highest form of staff development.

2. When teachers of various disciplines mix, creativity is enhanced.

3. The collected wisdom, creativity, and experience of any group of college instructors far surpass that of any one expert or speaker.

4. Success in teaching lies in the ability to teach a few ideas extremely well.

Each summer, community-college instructors, often the "Teacher of the Year" from many colleges, traveled to the coast of Maine to engage in some of the most rewarding seminars of their professional lives. Living for a week or two with fifty to one hundred master teachers was for many participants a stimulating highlight of their professional careers.

What went on during Garrison's National Master Teacher summer seminars? The faculty participants, each year from twenty-five to thirty states and up to seventy-five colleges, representing a wide variety of disciplines (from art to zoology, philosophy to welding) met to study ways to make their teaching more effective. It was a working seminar, designed to generate useful, relevant teaching ideas and techniques for each participant. There were no outside speakers, panels, or canned presentations, "no usual apparatus of passivity." Instead, working teams met daily to discuss common teaching problems and solutions. The agenda was created each day by the master teachers to meet their concerns, their questions, their interests as they had developed from the workshops and discussions of the days before. As Garrison so often said: There was no possibility of creating an agenda months in advance that, for ten days, would satisfy the hungry intelligence of a roomful of master teachers.

There were "miniworkshops," often extending two or three days, on specific matters such as how to individualize instruction in various ways, how to get students off to a good start, writing across the curriculum, how to handle different levels of student ability in the same classroom, how slowly and steadily to shift responsibility for learning to the learner, strategies for survival in a time of heavy teaching loads, strategies to teach adults (especially night students) differently from other students, and discussions of motivation, handling discipline problems, and preventing burn-out.

A lighter evening session might ask each teacher to offer two or three nonastounding teaching techniques—things that work well, but are not worth a published article or even a footnote. After such a session, a participant might have gathered two hundred or so hints for saving time or finding inexpensive materials, holding a more interesting class, etc., secrets discovered and shared by other teachers. Swell Teacher Clinics offered faculty (often isolated in their own classrooms) the rare opportunity to observe other excellent teachers teach, and these became a popular part of Garrison's seminars.

Each day, the seminar had a brief general meeting of the whole group, and then there were three seventy-five-minute workshops with occasional longer and more complex sessions. Evening sessions occasionally addressed areas of broad concern, such as teaching open admissions students, and several evenings were deliberately reserved for informal get-togethers: art shows, guitar or balalaika or bagpipe music, Japanese flower arrangements, even a magic show. The group's "hidden" talents were surprising.

When Garrison asked me to join the staff conducting the master teacher seminars, I humbly agreed. After his death, several of us carried on his approach until it seemed that most colleges and universities in the country were familiar with the master teacher seminar model as they spun off into workshops and retreats on hundreds of campuses around the country.

Garrison's influence can be seen today in the acceptance of the process approach to teaching writing, in the familiar use of the conference method in all its variations, and in the master teacher professional seminar/workshop response to staff development. Certainly, today's community-college teachers are often much better prepared for the challenging community-college students than were their teaching peers of the 1960s. Some of that preparedness can be traced to the efforts of Roger Garrison whose writings about teaching writing and whose approaches to staff development can still offer insights today.

With his larger-than-life personality, his intense insights, and his marvelous teaching, Garrison affected, directly or indirectly, thousands of community-college faculty. They, in turn, affected tens of thousands of community-college students. Thus, Garrison reaches us still.

## Chronological Bibliography of Roger H. Garrison's Work

### *Books*

Garrison, Roger H. 1951. *A Creative Approach to Writing.* New York: Holt.

———. 1959. *The Adventure of Learning in College: An Undergraduate Guide to Productive Study.* New York: Harper.

——. 1967. *Junior College Faculty: Issues and Problems; a Preliminary National Appraisal. Washington: Amer. Assoc. of Junior Colleges.*

——. 1968. *Teaching in a Junior College: A Brief Professional Orientation.* Washington: Amer. Assoc. of Junior Colleges.

——. 1974. *Implementing Innovative Instruction.* San Francisco: Jossey.

——. 1981, 1985. *How a Writer Works.* New York: Harper.

## Articles

(This list is limited to articles about education/writing and does NOT include Garrison's numerous contributions to contemporary magazines and newspapers.)

Garrison, Roger H. 1967. "Junior College Faculty—Issues and Problems, a Preliminary National Appraisal." ERIC EDO12177.

——. 1968. "Teaching in a Junior College, a Brief Professional Orientation." ERIC EDO22475.

——. 1968. "New Approaches to Teaching." ERIC EDO25539.

——. 1969. "1969 Seminar for Great Teachers." *Junior College Journal* 40.3: 7–9.

——. 1969. "What Students Want." *Improving College and University Teaching* 17.3: 149–50.

——. 1969. "Private Junior Colleges: The Question of Survival." *Junior College Journal* 39.6: 35–38.

——. 1971. "Morality, Sanity, and Colleges." *Improving College and University Teaching* 19.2: 104–05.

——. 1974. "One-to-One: Tutorial Instruction in Freshman Composition." *New Directions for Community Colleges* 2.1: 55–84.

——. 1975. "The Literature of the Two-Year Colleges." *Change* 7.3: 58–60.

——. 1975. "A Mini-Manual on In-Service." *Community and Junior College Journal* 45.9: 18–20.

——. 1976. "Tools of the Teaching Trade." *Improving College and University Teaching* 24.2: 68–71.

——. 1979. "Teaching English in the 1980's." *Teaching English in the Two-Year College* 5: 171–77.

——. 1981. "What Is an *A* Paper? A *B*? A *C*? A *D*?" *Teaching English in the Two-Year College* 7: 209–10.

# Works Cited

Dawe, C. W., and E. A. Dornan. 1997. *One to One Resources for Conference Centered Writing.* 5th ed. New York: Addison.

Koeppel, M. S. 1989. *Writing—Resources for Conferencing and Collaboration.* Englewood Cliffs: Prentice.

———. 2004. *Writing Strategies, Plus Collaboration.* 4th ed. Boston: Pearson.

Simmons, J. A. M. 1984. "The One-to-One Method of Teaching Composition." *College Composition and Communication* 35: 222–29.

# 10

## Developing a Writing Philosophy
### Elizabeth A. Nist

> Theory is autobiography. Exposition is narrative.
> —Louise Wetherbee Phelps

## Introduction

In 1991, I was selected to participate in the Minnesota Writing Project (MWP). As a recent transplant to the Midwest, it was a great opportunity for me, a veteran teacher from Utah, to network with new colleagues and explore new ideas about teaching. A final assignment of this summer institute was for each of us to draft a statement of our personal teaching philosophy. I thought this would be easy until I discovered it to be an assignment I could never finish. My teaching philosophy will always be a work-in-progress. At first, this was a discouraging discovery. I set aside my notes and gave up, until the next summer when I returned to the MWP as an Institute leader. There was that assignment again. It wouldn't . . . it won't . . . go away.

Lillian Bridwell-Bowles insisted, and I agree, that every teacher should draft a statement of teaching philosophy because this writing compels us to (1) describe the nature of writing and reading and how these are practiced in the classroom, (2) define the roles of teacher and student and the nature of these relationships, and (3) detail the goals of education and how students' achievement of these goals is assessed. A statement of teaching philosophy is essential to good teaching because it identifies the core values and beliefs on which we base our curriculum design, our classroom practice, and our professional conduct.

So, since 1991, I have been struggling to draft an accurate and meaningful statement of my teaching philosophy. In the process I've come to

98

understand the truth of Louise Wetherbee Phelps' comment, "Theory is autobiography; exposition is narrative" (vii).

A natural starting point for this self-examination seems to be a definition of the nature of writing and also reading. On reflection, I have come to realize that my philosophy as a writing teacher evolved along with my career as a two-year-college teacher.

## The 1950s and Traditionalism

My 1950s elementary education was parochial and traditional. I was taught reading and writing as basic skills; today, in many current documents on curriculum design, writing and reading are still described separately as basic skills. This is so because two major "camps" in our discipline seem comfortable with this term *skill*: many traditionalists and the cognitivists.

Traditionalists are willing to define writing and reading separately as basic skills because they focus on writing as a product (produced by the skilled). Reading is also a product (i.e., the correct interpretation of a text). Traditionalist teachers, whose philosophy is based on "positivism" or "scientism," equate knowledge with truth and with proof. Facts are context-free; they do not depend on their relations to other facts or on a situation where they function in a particular way, or on the interpretation of an observer (Phelps 9). Traditionalists value writing that is characterized by an "objective" attitude established by the "objective" language of the "neutral" scientist. The traditionalist (positivistic) ideology places knowledge in the domain of authorities who have the "truth." Teachers, by way of their education and training, have been initiated to this corps of authorities, the "academy." They position themselves at the centers of their classrooms as the masters who train unskilled apprentices, their students, in these *basic skills* of reading and writing.

The role of reading in traditional classrooms is to understand the voices of authorities recorded in texts (the texts of the canon). Student writing is the written recitation of the correct meaning of the text. The traditional teacher values (1) the third-person "objective" (usually voiceless) point of view, (2) form over content by stressing rhetorical modes as formal conventions, and (3) correctness over depth of thought. Good writing is "correct" writing at the sentence level; judgments are based mostly on form.

The advantage of this approach is efficiency. There are right and wrong answers. Consequently, writing and reading *skills* can be assessed by machine-scored tests. What is really being assessed here are vocabulary, reading speed, and editing *skills*.

In the traditional first-year composition course, the major (and generally unspoken) goal is to "civilize" undisciplined, un*skilled* student writers for the study of literature, so that these students might appreciate and respect the authorities they will eventually be able to read. Since the origins of composition as a required "gatekeeper" course at Harvard in 1874–75, composition has been perceived as a remedial subject. Mastery of the "basic skills" proved a candidate worthy of full matriculation as a university student. Following the Harvard model, nationalistic, abstract ideals of literary study soon dominated both the goal of and the justification for writing instruction (Miller 31). American colleges and universities taught writing about literature, if they taught writing at all.

At least two current works present a detailed account of the political history of composition: *Textual Carnivals* by Susan Miller and *Uncommon Sense* by John Mayher. Basing their analyses on years of research, both writers describe how defining writing and reading as basic skills is a conservative definition that values the status quo. Its goals are the preservation of present institutions and power structures and the indoctrination of a well-behaved body politic—worthy goals for the fully franchised.

But is it accurate to define writing as a *skill*? *Skill* is the name we give to proficiency in a craft, a trade, or a technique that requires the use of the hands or body. The word *skill* connotes physical rather than mental dexterity; the term *basic skills* implies the development of physical coordination necessary for normal living—swimming, riding a bicycle, driving an automobile. These are *basic skills*. To categorize writing and reading as basic skills denigrates writers and readers and promotes the remedial image attached to college reading and writing courses. Writing is not a *skill*. Penmanship and keyboarding are skills. Reading thoughtfully is not a *skill*. Writing and reading are extremely complex intellectual engagements.

The traditionalist's philosophy denies the possibility of a paradigm shift in Western culture, working instead to guarantee the continuance of positivism (or scientism) as the conceptual framework for knowledge (Phelps 60). Positivism insists that there are only two kinds of answers: right/wrong; good/bad; white/black. For the positivist there is no gray area. Truth is absolute.

This is how I was *taught* to read and write; this is not how I *learned* to read, to write, and to think.

## The 1960s and Expressivism

By the middle of my second year of college (1963), my self-confidence as a writer was thoroughly undermined. In November 1963, John Kennedy was assassinated. Perhaps it was the pervasive disillusionment of a generation. Perhaps it was my personal insecurity. It was probably all that and more. I was earning my own way through college working as a diet aide in a local hospital kitchen, and I weighed 180 pounds. It was time to get real about life; I transferred from a small, private, liberal arts college to San Fernando Valley State College (SFVSC) in Northridge, California. I abandoned my dream of being a writer and changed my major to dietetics. This was my first encounter with "public" education.

In June 1966, I received my B.S. degree in dietetics with minors in business administration and chemistry. On graduation day, I weighed a lean and healthy 120 pounds, and I was promoted to food service manager at the hospital where I had first trained as a diet aide and dishwasher.

If the California state college system had not offered me an opportunity to complete an affordable and solid undergraduate program, I don't know what might have happened. It was the Vietnam era. My daughter's birth, in April 1968, was bracketed by the assassinations of Martin Luther King, Jr., and Robert Kennedy.

My two-year-college teaching career began in 1969 when I was recruited by Moorpark College in California to teach foods and nutrition in the evening school. Meanwhile, I continued working full-time as a dietitian. At the same time, I went back to SFVSC to earn a vocational teaching credential and work toward an M.S. degree in human nutrition. Sometimes classes were interrupted by student riots, and we were evacuated from our apartment following the Northridge earthquake in February 1971. We had nothing to lose.

In the methods classes for the vocational certificate, group work was the core of classroom interaction: four students to a "kitchen," six kitchens to a lab. Demonstrate, discuss, practice, and evaluate—those were the four basic components of every lesson plan. It was a process approach, with lots of group work and student discussion, analysis, and evaluation of assignments. This was how I was taught to teach, and I liked teaching in the community college.

On the job, I was supervising sixty employees of all nationalities and races. Just as the community college has become an entry point for minorities to access higher education, a commercial kitchen is often an entry point for access to the workforce. Many new employees did not speak English at all. Then, I had to speak Spanish daily, and quickly became accustomed to conversations that included translators of other languages, including American Sign Language.

As I gained self-confidence, some financial stability, and professional expertise, my passion for writing resurfaced. In 1970, I registered for a poetry workshop taught by Ann Stanford at SFVSC (now California State University, Northridge).

Ann Stanford taught me to define creativity as the combining of known images in surprising ways to yield a sudden insight that resonates with truth and clarity. She emphasized the power of verbs to communicate specific, concrete detail. Writing began with a specific sensory image that aroused memory and suggested an array of complex connotations. This approach to writing was very different from what I had experienced in the past.

Ann Stanford introduced me to William Stafford, encouraging me to take some poetry workshops with him, and I registered for other writing courses as well. In fiction and playwriting workshops, we focused on memory, journal-keeping, and lots of (ungraded) writing. I developed fluency and personal voice. In these expressivist classrooms, the students were at the center, and writing was valued as a means of learning. These teachers held the view that creating text involves exploring personal experience and voice. The act of expression was (and is) both an embodiment and a clarification—an embodiment of a feeling already experienced, but whose form is not clarified until the act of expression is complete (Fishman 650). Assigned reading meant reading the work of other students in the class. The student became the subject exploring personal experience and voice; the teacher acted as the coach.

Reconnecting personal experience with writing aroused my strong reaction against the traditional methods of teaching writing that had alienated me from my own work as an undergraduate student. If writing doesn't illuminate personal experience, what's the point? That's the question students ask.

I had come out of the traditional writing classrooms of my high school and undergraduate years silenced. I had been denied the use of my own voice, and I had been prohibited from making connections between my personal experience and the content of the courses. Consequently, I found this encounter with expressivism freeing and exhilarating, but it didn't offer me any strategies for moving from this personal (creative) voice to an empowered public voice.

## The 1970s and Cognitivism

I did have authority in my field as a dietitian. In 1974, I sold my first article, "Cool-Rise Yeast Bread," to *Woman's Day*. By then I had moved from Los Angeles to Orem, Utah, where I was recruited to be the program coordinator for hotel and restaurant management at Utah Technical College. But I loved my work as a freelance writer, so I continued graduate work part-time—now studying for an M.A. in English at the University of Utah. By then I was publishing articles regularly, so relationships with editors supplemented relationships with professors as critical readers of my work. Editors demanded I revise with a keen sensitivity to the needs, values, and interests of my readers.

Meanwhile, in the 1970s, the focus shifted from product to process in many writing classrooms. Grounding themselves in cognitive psychology, cognitive rhetoricians claimed that there are three elements involved in composing: (1) the task environment, including such external constraints as the rhetorical problem and the text so far produced; (2) the writer's long-term memory (i.e., the knowledge of the subject considered and the knowledge of how to write); and (3) the writing process that goes on in the writer's mind. They also categorized the mental processes of writing into three stages:

- the planning stage, further divided into generating, organizing, and goal setting;
- the translating stage, the point at which thoughts are put into words;
- the reviewing stage, made up of evaluating and revising (Berlin 481).

The composition theory I was studying in graduate courses in English seemed to be making some connection to the methods I had been trained to use in teaching food service management: demonstrate, discuss, practice, evaluate.

Then, in 1977, the general education program at Utah Technical College underwent severe cutbacks in curriculum and funding. Separate disciplines were reorganized as a single "Department of General Education," and I was selected as the new chairperson. It was a challenging position.

Meanwhile, my husband, screenwriter Jack Nist, was working on a script, which was accepted for further development at Robert Redford's Sundance Institute for Independent Filmmakers. We were fortunate to spend June 1982 living at Sundance and working daily with some of the best writers, directors, and actors in the country.

Three major theoretical concepts became clear for me at Sundance: narrative structure, reader response theory, and the dynamics of group work for writers. I did a lot of thinking about writing while I was standing in a trout stream. My thoughts seemed to match the rhythm of the cast and the graceful movement of the line settling into a small, deep pool. I would come back to our cabin with my catch of the day, and while I panfried the fresh fish, I could listen to Jack talking with Hume Cronyn or Ed Herman about how an actor reads a script.

Actors are professional readers who give physical presence to the meaning they've constructed from the writer's words. Where there are gaps in the information the writer doesn't give about a character, the actor fills in with knowledge from his own experience. Each take might be a different reading. And while the director selects the take he wants— the "authoritative" reading— for a particular film, it was obvious that many "authoritative" readings were possible.

One day I watched Robert Duvall direct Wilford Brimley and Eddie Olmos through several scenes. Then they all switched roles, and Jack directed. It was a different film each time, even though the words spoken were the same. Each reading is an interpretation, a rendering of a text.

On another day we were invited to sit in on a session with Robert Redford and Doonesbury cartoonist Garry Trudeau, who were collaborating on a script for a political satire. They brainstormed and played with outrageous possibilities. They took their time. They also took risks—trying out any nuance of character, any twist of plot, or bit of dialogue, no matter how ridiculous. There were no critics there. The critics are invited to the premiere of the finished piece—they are never sitting across the desk from the professional writer composing.

While at Sundance, I learned how much writers need time—regular blocks of quiet time every day—to think, to read, and to write. We also need safe and inspiring places to talk about our writing—to take risks and try outrageous ideas. And we need different kinds of responses at different stages of a project. Finally, I learned how much collaboration professional writers do.

By this time I had completed my term as general education department chair; my full-time teaching assignment was in English: composition and literature. Personal computers were becoming available to students in open labs on campus. I was ready. I merged all I had learned about "process" strategies from my experiences teaching foods and nutrition, from my theory classes at Utah, and from the summer at Sundance. My classrooms became workshops where we practiced the writing process repeatedly. My students produced multiple drafts; I assumed the role of editor/director.

But, of course, I still responded to each of those drafts as my traditionalist colleagues expected, marking every error, and I required the students to do lots of journal writing as I had learned from my expressivist mentors. While the students' writing seemed to make more improvement with this new process approach, there were still some nagging problems.

The workload was nearly unmanageable. At the same time, some of the students grew bored with a process they found tedious. The textbooks tended to regiment the class into a rigid and linear process, not at all like the flexible, individual, recursive process I had experienced at Sundance. In addition, an annoying group of four to six students in every class thrived on writing the paper in a single draft hours before it was due. And there were also those troublesome two or three independent students who absolutely refused to participate in a group.

At this point I felt caught in a double-bind. On the one hand I was trying to implement the newest composition theories and the most current classroom practices. But as we discussed text adoptions and revised curriculum in department meetings, the "process model" often seemed to become the traditional "skills" approach redressed in process language. In assignments such as comparison/contrast papers, process papers, and extended definitions, form was valued over the content of student writing; technique was more important than thought. Sometimes the emphasis on procedure verged on "methodolatry"—it outlawed the students' exploring questions that could not be answered by the assigned method (Belenky 95-96). Even now, many texts that claim "process" in their titles and advertising, in fact, continue to require students to practice writing as a skill.

Meanwhile, I was thinking and writing through a much more fluid, recursive, global, and collaborative process. I had become part of an informal group of six writers who regularly exchanged and responded to one another's work.

In the face of these contradictory practices and the consequences they seemed to have on the diversity of learners in my classroom, I had to rethink the nature and purpose of writing (and reading) and the kinds of outcomes the students and I anticipated and valued.

## The 1980s and Social Constructionism

Graduate programs in composition and rhetoric began appearing in university bulletins. Across the country, college writing programs were divorcing themselves from English departments. The National Council of Writing Program Administrators and the Western States Writing Program Administrators became my bulwarks of professional support and development.

In 1988, Susan Miller recruited me for a temporary appointment as Writing 101 Coordinator at the University of Utah, where I worked most closely with Kathryn Fitzgerald. At the time, Susan was researching *Textual Carnivals: a Political History of Composition*, and Kathy Fitzgerald and Jamie McBeth Smith were drafting their new text, *The Student Writer*. Participating in frequent conversations about these works-in-progress along with the new experience of training TAs as teachers of writing expanded my perspectives. This was also the year *College English* published James Berlin's article, "Rhetoric and Ideology in the Writing Class," and I read *Women's Ways of Knowing* for the first time.

From this new vantage point, writing had to be defined as more than a process. I was not alone in this felt need. Since World War II, scientism has come under increased attack because of its inability as a framework to accommodate many questions raised by postmodern human experience. As Thomas Kuhn and many others have argued, this inability of scientism to explain observed and disturbing phenomena has caused philosophers and theorists across the disciplines to synthesize a new conceptual framework for knowledge.

The "new" or "renewed" discipline of composition and rhetoric has been participating actively in this revisioning of the nature of knowledge and, consequently, the nature of writing and reading. The hallways and seminar rooms at the University of Utah and national conference sessions were heated by philosophical debates in jargon denser than the inversion fog that settled into the Salt Lake Valley for months at a time.

The social constructionist movement, as I understand it, really came to this country with the English translation of Jacques Derrida's *Of Grammatology* in 1976. My grasp of this text and related works that comprise the complex network of social constructionist theory drove me toward defining my classroom as a discourse community.

The purpose of the work of Derrida and his followers is to "erase" (deconstruct) the doctrine of "presence" in Western metaphysics. Derrida asserts that traditional philosophy binds and distorts our thinking about the relations between self-consciousness, thought, and language; and that traditional thought about these matters promotes a number of powerful and yet unspoken assumptions that have "blinded" Westerners to the deceptive nature of speech and writing and their role in human activities. "Deconstruction" is Derrida's attempt to expose these assumptions for what they are. Consequently, he concentrates much of his attention on rereading the major texts of Western philosophy in an attempt to "unpack" the workings in them of what he calls "the metaphysics of presence." He demonstrates his theory with close readings of the works of thinkers such as Edmund Husserl, Immanuel Kant, and Sigmund Freud (Crowley xvi).

Before Derrida, western theories about writing had been author-centered (i.e., based on the assumption that the writing process begins and ends with an individual author—a sovereign, self-aware consciousness—at the center of any composing act). Therefore, writing research focused primarily on authors, specifically on their intentions and psychology. Writing had been viewed as the exterior representation of the author's interior thought.

In contrast, deconstructionists focus on language, because (they claim) it both precedes and succeeds individual writers. Thus, a deconstructive attitude toward writing pedagogy focuses attention away from individual authors—away from process and toward transaction—toward the language currently in use in the community and how writers and readers construct meaning with that language.

Consequently, we hear the term "social constructionist" applied to those who argue that good writers and readers must master the accepted practices of a discourse community. What we read is writing, not thought. But these theorists themselves do not share much with each other in the way of basic tenets, common definitions, or universal values and beliefs—except, possibly, their argument that there are no "universal truths."

The ferment that resulted from my own immersion in poststructuralist theory has shaken me with some unnerving insights into my own teaching practices. First, I came to realize that teachers do most of the writing in traditional composition classes, while the students are more often passive readers. We write the syllabus, the assignments, and the daily lesson plans; we rewrite the textbook in the sense that we interpret it for the students; and, finally, we write (revise, edit, grade) our students' papers. Students, on the other hand, spend most of their time reading: they "read" the teacher, the textbooks, and the assignments. When they "write," their purpose is usually to tell teachers what they think we want to hear. Almost never do they envision themselves as having something to say that is new, informative, or insightful for us as readers.

Again I revised my teaching methods. Now students not only select their own topics, but they also identify the target audience with whom they want to share their ideas. They do not assume that I am their only reader; and, as often as not, the writing is presented, one way or another, to the intended audience. In this way students experience writing as more than an academic exercise completed for critique and evaluation. Their writing is an act of authentic communication with a real purpose and a real audience.

Second, classroom writing is to be collaborative and contextual in its composition; so then, (theoretically) it is available to anyone who can read it. This theoretic availability can be realized in practice when students are encouraged to immerse their classroom writing into the flow of whatever public discourse is going on around them—in their college, workplaces, communities, or on the Internet. In fact, the dissemination of classroom writing into the discourse of the school or larger community is a solution to the difficulty that haunts much student writing, its lack of motivation.

"Deconstructing" the process model of the 1970s resulted in a third realization: Traditional pedagogy assumes that thinking precedes writing. Derrida's comments on this process come about in the context of his discussion of the puzzle of the preface, the part of the text that announces itself as coming before the text, yet is ordinarily written after the text is finished. The preface claims to embody or summarize or at least to introduce what is contained in the rest of the work.

In a deconstructive model of the writing process, we see how beginnings, middles, and endings are not quite so clearly delineated. The words written first may be the writer's entrance to the writing situation, but they may not be the best entrance for the reader. The writer's conclusions may be the reader's most effective "beginning." Texts ebb and flow, open and close, come and go. This fluidity of text is further enhanced today by computer technology.

This open-endedness, this ambiguity of intention or outcome, is not unusual. Just as often, the genre is prescribed by the nature of the writing situation itself: a letter of recommendation, a proposal, a memo, a report, a journal article, or the like. However, even when the genre is a given, I must also consider my experiences with the subject in question as well as the experiences and questions my readers have and their expectations of form in the context where my writing will be read. I have to balance all of these constraints of purpose, audience, context, and experience and use whatever resources I have at hand while I write.

Most importantly, a deconstructive attitude renders the notion of "expository writing" problematic. A writer who undertakes the composition of expository discourse must understand the subject under discussion better than the readers do. In exposition, the aim is to make others see the meaning of some idea as clearly as the writer sees it. How can students succeed when they are always writing for readers who know the topic better than they do? Derrida's critique suggests that when we writing teachers require our students to compose balanced, coherent, and organized essays on assigned topics, we set tasks that are impossible for students to accomplish.

First of all, assignments in exposition, if taken seriously, place students in the position of imitating writers who have devoted their careers to becoming expert in some discipline or specialized area of research. Such assignments at the very least, trivialize the difficult process of acquiring knowledge. But even more seriously, such assignments ask students to learn to manage the terms and conventions of the discourse that surrounds the "subject" in a very short time and without assistance.

"Successful" students, who have learned to play this game with us, work their way out of this dilemma by going to the library, where they collect and photocopy all the sources they can find. Then they "cut and paste" these sources together in a "balanced," "coherent," and "logical" pattern of organization with some kind of obvious structure (which may or may not have been stipulated by the assignment). In their imitation of the experts, students are constantly hounded by the temptation to plagiarize these sources who are so much more knowledgeable and articulate than they. Nevertheless, they forge ahead to draft a thesis statement and introduction to paste at the top of their "text" and a conclusion at the bottom. The teacher's grade on the assignment is really a comment on the quality of the "glue" the students have written—how well the pieces hold together. The students' papers are, in fact, annotated bibliographies, which we discuss and evaluate as expository writing and, even worse, as research.

In contrast, social constructionists view their classrooms as "discourse communities" composed of teacher and students who interact with one another as equal participants in the creation of knowledge through dialogue. Reading is defined as dialogue with a text; the reader recomposes the text. Writing classes taught by social constructionists concentrate on dialectic (critical thinking) and value the argument that persuades the group. Consequently, a pivotal assignment in this kind of course is the documented argument. But feminists argue that argument is a masculine approach to problem solving, which is easily subverted to the dualistic thinking of the traditionalist. Dialogue becomes a two-sided debate with a winner and a loser. Feminist rhetoricians are committed to affirming ordinary life and the potential of ordinary people for reflection and participation in the conversation of humankind (Phelps 56). So even on this pivotal assignment, social constructionists do not all agree.

Many two-year-college teachers have been put off by the jargon of deconstruction, which often appears elitist to us. Furthermore, for the introvert, the teaching methods of social constructionists seem to overvalue collaboration, often ignoring the preferred learning and writing styles of introverts, those few students in every class who balk at collaboration. Furthermore, in the real context of two-year-college teaching loads, collaborative portfolio assessment has also been controversial even though it has been highly valued by social constructionists for many sound reasons.

## The 1990s and a Personal Philosophy

My personal philosophy has evolved as a synthesis of all these experiences. Since that first Minnesota Writing Project Summer Institute, my two-year-college classrooms have become workshops for writers. My role is editor/facilitator assisting writers to accomplish their goals with their readers. We spend a lot of class time writing and discussing our writing. We take risks and explore new strategies and technologies and ideas. I encourage the students to engage in authentic and original research to answer real questions that are important to them, and then write their findings to an audience who shares their interest in their topic. Sometimes students will collaborate on larger projects.

For example, over a three-year period a couple hundred students collected and wrote the oral history of Coon Rapids, the community where our campus is located. This research project was designed and coordinated in collaboration with the Coon Rapids Historical Commission. The student papers were compiled as a 600-page manuscript presented together with copies of audiotaped interviews and transcripts to the Historical Commission. The students found the power and value of their public voices; the community gained a new respect for student research and writing. This project is only one example of the kinds of authentic research that students can experience. It is important to note that participation was voluntary, and this was also a multimedia project.

It is becoming increasingly important to recognize that visual and oral communications are as legitimate and permanent as written communications; visual literacy may become more valued than verbal literacy for the next generation. Even now we can demonstrate how, when a "reader" is presented with visual and verbal messages simultaneously, the visual message will have more immediate and lasting impact than the verbal—every time! How we communicate is becoming much more integrated; writers and readers are becoming more interactive within the text. This means that if we are to teach composition, we must explore thoroughly with students how meaning is constructed visually and verbally among writers and their audiences.

I've tried out all these definitions of writing/reading: as basic skills, as self-discovery, as process, and as the construction of knowledge. But as my colleague Larry Barton wrote for the Minnesota Writing Project, these various philosophical positions are like the old story of four blind men describing an elephant. Each has a partial image, but none grasps the larger truth. I'm left wondering how much of the "elephant" we have not yet explored.

At the same time I find it curious that the four current ideologies dominant in composition and rhetoric—with their four different definitions of reading and writing—seem to parallel the four stages of women's cognitive development:

- received knowledge: listening to the voices of authorities
- subjective knowledge: the inner voice and the quest for self
- procedural knowledge: the voice of reason; separate and connected knowing
- constructed knowledge: integrating the voices (Belenky, et al.).

Is this simply coincidence? Or is my personal development proof of this research? Or has composition and rhetoric as an academic discipline followed a "feminine" and natural pattern of maturation? Or did the women studied by Belenky and her colleagues happen to grow up (as I have) through these periods of evolution in pedagogical theory, so their ways of knowing reflect the ways they were being taught? Even more important, could the coincidence of these same patterns of development imply that we should use a traditional approach to teach reading and writing in the elementary levels, an expressivist approach at the secondary level, a cognitive approach at the undergraduate level, and a social constructionist approach with graduate students? Should we integrate all these approaches to teaching rather than continuing to describe them as separate, often hostile, ideologies? Future research may show that all of these approaches have an appropriate place in education.

Nevertheless, I need a working definition of writing/reading now. I cannot continue to value the application of all these theories simultaneously in my community-college classroom. Their contradictory demands make this impossible. Yet, while I find some value in each perspective, I see their disadvantages, too. I cannot wholly embrace any one of them. Instead, I must integrate what I've learned from each with my own experience, to synthesize a coherent and personal philosophy of teaching.

At the epicenter, as the result of many years of teaching in two-year-college classrooms, I have come to define writing and reading together as essentially human interaction with the purpose of bridging absence via a system of recorded symbols.

I choose my own category of "human interaction" very deliberately here. To write and read is essentially human—the writer encodes meaning; the reader decodes. We write notes, memos, and letters to readers who are absent at the moment of writing. We write history to future generations. We write journals and notes to our future selves who need to be reminded of a present thought, impression, or experience that may too soon be forgotten or changed by the passage of time. We write to think because we have a limited consciousness that cannot be omnipresent to the complexity of elements we are attempting to analyze or synthesize. We write to learn because the mass of human experience has far outstripped the data bank of a single human mind. We can no longer intellectually possess and pass on all we know through an oral tradition. We write to delight because human interaction always carries the potential for intimacy and arousal, pain and ecstasy. We write to know one another and ourselves. And for all the same reasons that we write, we also read: to think, to learn, to delight, and to know one another.

# Works Cited

Belenky, M. F., et al. 1986. *Women's Ways of Knowing: The Development of Self, Voice, and Mind.* New York: Harper.

Berlin, J. 1988. "Rhetoric and Ideology in the Writing Class." *College English* 50: 477–94.

Crowley, S. 1989. *A Teacher's Introduction to Deconstruction.* Urbana: NCTE.

Derrida, J. 1976. *Of Grammatology*. Translated by Gayatri Chakravorty Spivak. Baltimore: Johns Hopkins UP.

Fishman, S. M., and L. P. McCarthy. 1992. "Is Expressivism Dead? Reconsidering Its Romantic Roots and Its Relations to Social Constructionism." *College English* 54: 647-63.

Fitzgerald, K. R., and J. McB. Smith. 1991. *The Student Writer*. New York: Harper.

Kuhn, T. 1970. *The Structure of Scientific Revolutions*. 2nd ed. Chicago: U Chicago P.

Mayher, John S. 1990. *Uncommon Sense. Theoretical Practice in Language Education*. Portsmouth: Boynton.

Miller, S. 1991. *Textual Carnivals. The Politics of Composition*. Carbondale: Southern Illinois UP.

Phelps, L. W. 1988. *Composition as a Human Science: Contributions to the Self-Understanding of a Discipline*. New York: Oxford UP.

# 11

## Reminiscing about a Two-Year Regional Conference: Two Voices/One Viewpoint

### Ann Laster and Beverly Fatherree

## Introduction

Ann Laster, with over thirty-five years as an educator and participant in NCTE's Southeast two-year-college regional organization, and Beverly Fatherree, with over twenty-five years of experience with the group, collaborate on their views of the two-year-college regionals and their personal involvement with the Southeast regional. Ann was present almost from the beginning; Beverly came in after the structure was in place. Both, however, agree on the importance of the organization in the development of their careers, their teaching philosophies, and their professional liaisons, which are so critical in keeping abreast of the trends in teaching and in the discipline of English studies. They reminisce about experiences with NCTE's Southeast organization for two-year English instructors, from 1965 to 1994 labeled the Southeastern Conference on English in the Two-Year College (SCETC), and since 1994, the Two-Year College English Association-Southeast (TYCA-Southeast). In discussing the role of SCETC in their professional growth, they suggest the importance of all the NCTE regional conferences in the professional lives of thousands of two-year-college teachers across the country.

**Ann**: When I began teaching at Hinds Junior College (now Hinds Community College) in Raymond, Mississippi, in 1964, I regularly attended state conferences for English teachers and national conferences of the National Council of Teachers of English and the Conference on College Composition and Communication. In 1968, I attended my first two-year regional English conference in Biloxi, Mississippi, and became a member of SCETC. Since 1968, I've attended SCETC annual conferences, served in various leadership positions, and found they consistently provide mountain-high personal and professional satisfaction and invaluable professional development.

**Beverly:** When Ann was attending her first SCETC conference in Biloxi in 1968, I was finishing up my junior year in high school. After graduating, I enrolled in Hinds Junior College, about thirty miles from my home in Vicksburg. I won't say that Hinds was my first choice of school, but because my parents already had one child in college and would soon have three when my sister graduated the year after me, it was just about my only choice. Soon, though, I realized what a wonderful place Hinds was and fell in love with everything about it. The teachers were excellent, the social life active, and the educational opportunities superb. When I graduated two years later and went on to Millsaps College with the smoothest of transitions and a scholarship, I knew that one day I wanted to return to Hinds to teach. And return I did, in 1980. To say that I was wet behind the ears is an understatement; at that point I had taught three semesters of freshman composition as a graduate assistant and one year of high school English. I had much to learn, and luckily I was among teachers who were willing to guide me.

# Historical Background

**Ann:** When I attended the 1968 SCETC annual meeting, the organization had only held two previous meetings. Organized formally in 1966 at Central Piedmont Community College in Charlotte, North Carolina, the Southeast conference was one of six regional conferences on English in the two-year college: Pacific Northwest, the Pacific Coast, the Southwest, the Midwest, the Northeast, and the Southeast, which included Alabama, Florida, Georgia, Mississippi, North Carolina, South Carolina, Tennessee, and Virginia. Later Kentucky and West Virginia were added to the Southeast.

The regionals actually began in 1965 with the National Junior College Committee of the Conference on College Composition and Communication coordinating the six regional conferences on English in the two-year college. In September 1966, the executive boards of NCTE and CCCC named a Director for the Two-Year-College English Program to serve as liaison between the two-year-college conferences and NCTE/CCCC. Organized to "provide a framework for a variety of professional activities among the teachers of English in two-year colleges within its region," each conference had additional specific goals:

- to define and explore issues relevant to the improvement of the teaching of English in the two-year colleges within its region,

- to conduct an annual regional conference,
- to publish materials containing reports of the regional conferences and news items of special interest to members within its region,
- to encourage studies and research in the teaching of English in the two-year colleges. (*By-Laws* 1965)

The regionals gave hope to two-year-college teachers and their institutions, which in the 1960s had somewhat nebulous identities. I can remember my early years as a junior-college teacher feeling that junior-colleges were almost nonentities. Their existence was minimally acknowledged but hardly respected. High school teachers and administrators saw them as a catchall for those too academically weak to attend universities or too lazy or unskilled to enter the workforce. University faculties' general perception was often that students who went to two-year colleges were not prepared academically to attend four-year colleges and/or that the instruction at the two-year colleges was not college level.

In 1965, the National Council of Teachers of English published *English in the Two-Year College*, a report of a joint committee of NCTE and the Conference on College Composition and Communication. The report published the results of a survey of 479 English teachers in 239 two-year colleges. Questions such as the following were asked: What is the two-year college? What is taught in the two-year college? What qualifications do teachers have? What unique problems exist? (Weingarten). This survey led to a major historical event for two-year colleges—the first national conference, held in Tempe, Arizona, in 1965, for dialogue between junior college and university teachers on professional issues. The Tempe conference brought together seventy representatives of English teachers and administrators in two- and four-year colleges, researchers, and officers of national agencies and associations. The challenges facing the two-year colleges, including the establishment of two-year colleges at a startling rate, the explosive increase in enrollment, the efforts to reform English curriculum, and the preparation of two-year-college English teachers, were discussed (Archer 1–5). The meeting addressed the issue that faced the two-year college in the 1960s and into the next decade. Who were we? How did we "fit" into the higher education hierarchy?

In 1968–1969, The Carnegie Corporation of New York funded a joint project of The Modern Language Association (MLA), NCTE, and The American Association of Junior Colleges (AAJC) entitled *The National Study of English in the Junior College*. The project report cited the coming of age of the two-year college in the 1960s and the resulting attention to two-year-college teachers, students, and curriculum.

Obviously, the attention of NCTE, CCCC, and MLA indicated an emerging national interest in the teaching of English in the two-year colleges. Two-year colleges would not go away; they would be heard.

In 1994, the NCTE's regional two-year organizations made another significant step. After numerous meetings of a nationally representative group of two-year-college teachers along with representatives from CCCC and NCTE, a plan evolved leading to a name change and a new role for the regionals. They became known as two-year-college English associations with the geographic designation included, i.e., the Two-Year College English Association-Southeast or TYCA-Southeast. Of great importance at this time was securing the participation of California's community colleges in the National TYCA organization when the English Council of California Two-Year Colleges agreed to become a TYCA regional, TYCA-Pacific Coast. The realignment then made for seven regionals, with Arizona, Hawaii, Nevada, and Utah becoming TYCA-West. Another achievement as a result of the establishment of National TYCA is that two-year teachers who join NCTE can now choose with their membership the journal *Teaching English in the Two-Year College* (*TETYC*). In 2002, the chair of National TYCA became an official voting member of the NCTE Executive Committee. These changes gave the two-year-college members much stronger representation at the national level. Even the Modern Language Association, in 1997, created a Committee on Community Colleges, further evidencing the importance of the two-year college on the national scene.

**Beverly:** I was one of the many who benefited from all of this hard work at the organizational level. By the time I came along, community-college teachers were a force to be reckoned with. Hinds was the second largest postsecondary institution in the state, behind only Mississippi State University. As more students began attending college, the community colleges were seen as necessary components to the education of many of the students who would have been deemed "not college material" just a decade before. Having attended both a two-year college and a top private four-year college, I knew the caliber of instruction that had prepared me for the degree in English I received at Millsaps and for further instruction in graduate school. As a young teacher, I was eager to be part of that tradition of excellence.

I attended my first SCETC convention in 1981, the spring after I was hired at Hinds Community College. Colleagues Polly Marshall, Retta Porter, Nell Ann Pickett, and Ann Laster told me that I should go to this conference, which ironically enough was meeting again in Biloxi. I was a novice in so many ways, but I piled into the car with Polly and Retta—and a suitcase full of far too many clothes (a problem I still have when attending a conference)—and headed to the Royal D'Iberville Hotel for my very first professional conference. With that trip, my professional life was transformed. (My personal life underwent some changes, too, just by virtue of six uninterrupted driving hours with Polly and Retta, but that's a story for another time.)

I was immediately mesmerized—by the people, the programs, the scholarship, and the fun. I attended sessions on technical writing, on sense of place in Eudora Welty's fiction, on holistic grading. All were lively with stimulating and useful information, and best of all, audience participation and question/answer segments. I saw Hinds' own Ray Shepherd receive the group's first Cowan Award for her teaching excellence (an award named for Gregory Cowan, longtime faculty member at Forest Park Community College in St. Louis). I attended the Friday evening banquet that featured a speaker unable to perform because of overindulgence (noteworthy to a young teacher because it was my first but not my last encounter with the foibles of the writers about whom I had studied and whose works I now taught in the classroom). I met colleagues who became dear friends. That conference, for me, was an introduction to the best of professional life, a life that extends beyond classroom or conference session into personal development, personal encouragement, and personal fulfillment.

## A Sense of Identity

**Ann:** With a fertile background of discussion, research, and data, NCTE's two-year regionals were born and have grown and thrived. The Southeast and the six other regionals have figured prominently in cementing the identity of the two-year college and its place in education.

Of course, those of us teaching in two-year colleges knew who we were from the beginning. We were first and foremost teachers in the trenches working with students who had the widest range of abilities and interests. With an open-door admission policy, two-year colleges attracted students with varied backgrounds: those wanting to change careers, parents and military personnel returning to school, workers upgrading skills, high school graduates feeling unprepared academically for a university, and varied students seeking affordable higher education. Many enrolled at two-year colleges after unsuccessful attempts at four-year colleges and universities. Our doors were open to them all. During my two-year-college teaching (1964–1997), I experienced the excitement and the frustrations resulting from the open-door policy, both of which generated innovative curricula and creative teaching techniques.

It was at the regional conferences that two-year-college English teachers shared their experiments, innovations, successes, and failures. SCETC and the other regionals became a hotbed of ideas and latest trends. Programmed instruction, modular learning, behavioral objectives, multimedia, honors programs, technical communication, ESL, academically disadvantaged students, the process approach to writing, prewriting heuristics, attention to audience and revision, writing across the curriculum, reader response, accountability, learning styles, writing assessment—these topics and many more showed up on programs for regional conferences. Conference participants flocked to the sessions, eager to listen, learn, share, and then try out new ideas in their classrooms. And because the meetings were usually small, with 200–300 members attending each year, there was an intimacy, a friendliness, and a full opportunity to participate.

My college was an early leader in providing a model for behavioral objectives, technical communication, and placement testing. At SCETC conferences, English faculty from Hinds presented programs on these topics, and our faculty members were on the telephone following up with colleagues interested in these subject areas and inviting teachers we had heard at the conferences to come to Hinds to tell us more about their experiences. Attending SCETC meetings allowed Hinds' instructors to share and to learn from peers about teaching diverse students, teaching new subject matter such as technical writing, and to develop new programs such as ESL, writing labs, and tutorial instruction. The regionals have provided an invaluable forum for two-year-college English teachers, a fact I know not only from the experience of participating in some fourteen SCETC conferences but also from reading program booklets, housed in the conference archives under my care for twenty years as the organization's archivist.

## Service and Inspiration

**Ann**: In May 1997, I retired after forty years of teaching, thirty-three of those years at Hinds. During those years I grew professionally as a result of service to SCETC in many roles.

My first participation on a program was in Birmingham in 1971. Nell Ann Pickett, my colleague at Hinds, and I, along with Don Rigg of Broward Junior College in Florida, made up a panel on technical English programs, chaired by David Comer, Georgia Institute of Technology. I was nervous to be speaking before a group of peers for whom I had great respect. Though I had much experience in teaching technical English, and though Nell Ann Pickett and I had published a textbook for introductory technical communication courses in 1970, I had some apprehension about speaking. While memory and the passing of time often make things better, I recall that the session was well received. And in the future there were many other opportunities to serve as panel speaker, recorder, or presider at annual conferences.

I left the Jacksonville, Florida, conference in 1973 as the designated local arrangements chair for the 1974 Jackson, Mississippi, conference. Thus began a different kind of involvement with SCETC. For
the next twenty-three years I would have very specific responsibilities.
From 1975 to 1977, I was elected to serve as chair of the Regional
Executive Committee (REC), the first person to serve a three-year term.
Serving on the REC gave me such respect for two-year-college teachers as we worked together to continue SCETC's growth as a viable,
meaningful organization. I learned of the unselfishness of two-year colleagues willing to support the regional organization with money and
in-kind services. The annual conferences in those early years enjoyed
significant support from two-year colleges throughout the Southeast
as they rotated annual meetings among major cities in the nine states
in the region.

The REC has always been concerned about membership, thus making an early decision to schedule annual meetings at strategic geographic
locations throughout the region so that all two-year-college teachers in
the Southeast would periodically have easy access to a meeting. With
every meeting, the goal has been to plan and present the best possible
program and social activities. In addition, planning and working on
annual meetings provided invaluable experiences to many two-year faculty members from those colleges that hosted an annual meeting or
planned the program. Many of these moved on to take leadership roles
in national professional organizations.

**Beverly**: When I joined the organization in 1981, the conference was
smoothly run by people who had worked long and hard to move it to the
level of professional respect it enjoyed from both two-year and four-year
teachers. For the first several conferences, I was merely an attendee, supporting colleagues, making friends, and learning the ropes. In Atlanta in
the early 1980s, I vigorously campaigned for my Hinds colleague, Jerry
Carr, who was a successful candidate for the REC. By 1986, I was on
the assistant program committee for Memphis; that involvement gave
me the courage to read for the first time at the open mike poetry/prose
session. And in 1987, I served on the program committee for the Jackson, Mississippi, conference. Under Nell Ann Pickett's direction, I
worked hard, but the rewards were many: the opportunity to introduce
writer Ellen Gilchrist, a featured speaker, to escort Eudora Welty to a
luncheon in her honor, to "hang out" with Will D. Campbell and Willie
Morris, both featured speakers, and to appreciate fully the strength and
camaraderie of SCETC.

And speaking of camaraderie, in 1988, Faye Barham and I edited
the second edition of the SCETC literary journal, *Camaraderie*. We put

out the third edition in 1992, and we're currently working on the fourth edition. *Camaraderie* has given SCETC members the opportunity to express themselves creatively through their poetry and fiction.

A natural outgrowth of my involvement with the programs at the annual meetings was being elected to the REC in 1996. I served one year as membership chair and two as member-at-large and Cowan Award Chair. My service at the regional level then led to national service with the Two-Year College English Association.

## Professional Development and Inspiration

**Ann:** SCETC not only opened doors for service to the profession, it also opened doors to me as a person and as a professional, and to my colleagues at Hinds. Inspiration at a conference event often led to improved classroom activities, encouragement to write and publish, and to appearances of outstanding speakers and literary figures on our campus, whom we invited after hearing them at a regional conference.

I learned so much about my special interest, technical communication, at SCETC conferences. I remember a presentation entitled "The Missing Half" by Gerald Cohen of IBM, who insisted that visuals were fifty percent of the meaning of a document. I first heard Don Cunningham present a session on the "so-what's" of technical communication, which stressed the practicality of technical writing. These now seemingly obvious insights into technical communication have had a major effect on my thinking, teaching, and writing.

In 1981, the Institute of Technical Communication held its initial gathering on the Mississippi Gulf Coast. At an earlier SCETC meeting in Birmingham, Alabama, Nell Ann Pickett, Dixie Hickman, and a group of interested persons decided such a workshop on technical writing should begin. And begin it did with sponsorship and financial support from SCETC. I served on the faculty for that initial Institute and continued until 2001. From 1986 until 2001, I was codirector with Penny Sansbury, Florence-Darlington Technical College, South Carolina, and from 1999, with Penny and Faye Barham, Hinds Community College. In 2001, the Institute moved to the Myrtle Beach Campus of Horry-Georgetown Technical College in South Carolina under the direction of Mike Williams, Horry-Georgetown, and Andrew Halford, Paducah Community College, Kentucky. What a growth experience working with the Institute was, not only for me but for the hundreds of high school, two-year, and four-year-college teachers, technical writers, and publishers' representatives from across the United States and Canada who have attended. The Institute directly grew from the Southeast two-year regional and remains the longest running such workshop, and the only one still active, focused exclusively on technical communication.

And there was inspiration on another level. I sat spellbound at an SCETC conference and listened to James Dickey read a poem about his young daughter. Not too long afterward, he walked onto the stage in Cain Hall on Hinds' Raymond campus. Wearing a Panama hat and a baggy blue coat and carrying a ragged suitcase full of books, he selected a volume and began to speak and read, weaving his spell over a thousand students and guests crammed into an 850-seat auditorium.

Virginia Spencer Carr captured the hearts of those who heard her at an SCETC conference tell about her research for the Dos Passos biography; her sense of humor and her scholarship impressed us all. A few months after speaking at SCETC, she came to Hinds for three days as writer-in-residence.

Attending SCETC conferences has given members the opportunity to rub shoulders with the giants in the field: Eudora Welty, Cleanth Brooks, Lee Smith, James McCrimmon, Gregory Cowan, Rick Bragg, Jesse Stuart, James Dickey, E.R. Braithwaite, Maxine Hairston, Dori Sanders, Peter Elbow, and John Berendt, among others. And we ourselves feel like giants as we meet together at annual conferences each winter, discussing common issues, realizing that we share common problems that can be solved. We know that we are not alone no matter the predicament, be it professional development, students, or curriculum. This common bond continues and gives us strength.

**Beverly**: The conferences have given me the opportunity to present programs, many with Faye Barham, my Hinds colleague, on a variety of subjects ranging from Southern women writers and the civil rights movement (with the late Betty Furstenberger) to the grotesque in Southern literature to alternate texts in teaching (with Jean Bridges) to the family as place in selected works of Lee Smith. At the 2000 conference in Savannah, I presented a one-woman show on Flannery O'Connor, and Faye and I are already at work on future offerings. We have presented several of these programs at national conferences as well, been invited to speak at other colleges, at library programs, and at our own institution because of the work generated for the Southeast conference.

For two years I also worked as an assistant editor for *Teaching English in the Two-Year College*, an opportunity that arose from my work with SCETC. And because of my association with community-college teaching, I've had two articles published in that journal.

The other rewards of membership in the organization are many. I've had the pleasure of introducing Ann Beattie, Rheta Grimsley Johnson, and our own Nell Ann Pickett at various conferences; I've had the privilege of publishing in the regional journal, the *TYCA-Southeast Journal*; I've presented programs at national conferences, programs always presented first at TYCA-Southeast. But my first choice for professional endeavor is always TYCA-Southeast. For one thing, the categories for presentation include literature, allowing me to indulge my passion for Southern writers without necessarily tying the presentation to composition. And I can always count on having friends at my presentation, ready to cheer me on and offer suggestions. Looking out at an SCETC audience is like looking at the members of my family, those I see at the reunion once a year.

## So What?

**Ann:** While many things have changed in the Southeast regional conference over the past thirty years (in 1969 dues were $1.50 and registration for that year's Atlanta meeting was $3.50; in 1994 SCETC became TYCA-Southeast; we recently added West Virginia to the regional), some things never change: The heart of SCETC/TYCA-Southeast has been its people, close as family, with a family's share of sweetness and sadness. In his "Chair's Note," Charles Smires wrote in the Spring 1998 *TYCA-Southeast Journal* about "eight 'sails' . . . that keep our organization not only afloat but moving forward!":

- Creativity, the promotion and celebration of the creative word and of innovative methodologies, approaches, and resources in the classroom.
- Family, the sense of belonging to a group of individuals who truly care about one another and who share in each other's successes, accomplishments, disappointments, and losses.
- Heritage, the celebration and preservation of the Southern literary tradition and voice.
- Leadership, the opportunity for and encouragement of members to become a leading voice in two-year-college instruction.
- Pride, the value and respect we hold for our two-year colleges that we work to instill in our students and our communities.
- Recognition, the acknowledgment of contributions of our members, whether full-time or adjunct, to our students, to our discipline, to our colleges, to our organization.
- Scholarship, the love we have for the pursuit of knowledge gained through study and research and the sharing of that knowledge in the classroom and through articles and presentations.
- Service, the opportunity to take an active role in promoting and enhancing two-year-college instruction throughout the Southeast and the nation. (3)

These "sails" propel not only the Southeast regional but all the two-year-college regionals and explain why they have been so important in the lives and professional development of thousands of two-year-college faculty members for the past thirty-eight years.

**Beverly**: Being a part of the Southeast regional has allowed me to incorporate all of the things mentioned in Charles Smires' excellent article into both my personal and my professional life. I have a unique opportunity to see the importance of an organization such as TYCA-Southeast to a teacher because my husband and my sister both teach at Hinds Community College, in history and in math, respectively. Neither has a regional organization of the caliber of TYCA-Southeast, and neither has the opportunity to have the professional involvement I have. They have both expressed their envy, especially every February when I pack those many bags to journey to Savannah or Fort Lauderdale or Richmond for the next conference. I always come home tired but happy, full of a sense of well-being and validation for myself as a teacher and as a professional. What more could we ask for as professionals in a field that is often underpaid, usually underrated, and always overworked.

# Closing

**Ann:** In a 1966 article Don Tighe, Valencia Community College, Florida, wrote of four concerns various individuals had expressed about beginning a regional conference:

1. Little conviction that regionals would be successful
2. Virtually no money with which to carry on the activities of the organization
3. Virtually no experience in planning or carrying out a conference
4. Virtually no sound plan for carrying on the activities of such an organization.

Tighe commented, "I was, to tell the truth, so naïve that I didn't share the convictions of many that these were problems to approach with great trepidation." And how right Don was.

The two-year-college regionals. What do they mean? The glow from hugs and kisses from friends, meeting new professional colleagues, and making new friends. The assurance of program sessions on the latest professional issues close to home. The opportunities for professional growth and networking with colleagues. A regional publication filled with information about the organization and the profession. The excitement of meeting national leaders in the profession and prominent writers. Opportunities to serve the profession, acquire leadership skills, and develop as a two-year-college English professional. An annual "family" reunion.

**Beverly**: AMEN!

# Works Cited

Archer, J. W., Director. 1965. *Research and the Development of English Programs in the Junior Colleges*. Proceedings of the Tempe Conference 1965. Champaign: NCTE.

*By-Laws of the Regional Conferences on English in the Two-Year College*. 1965. Urbana: NCTE.

*By-Laws of the Regional Conferences on English in the Two-Year College*. 1971. Urbana, NCTE.

The Modern Language Association, The National Council of Teachers of English, and The American Association of Junior Colleges. 1968–1969. *The National Study of English in the Junior College*. A Focus Report Published by the MLA ERIC Clearinghouse on the Teaching of English in Higher Education.

Smires, C. 1998. "Chair's Note." *TYCA-Southeast Journal*. (Spring): 3.

Tighe, D. Newspaper article, n.d. SCETC Archives.

Vickers, O., and A. Laster. 1990. *SCETC: A History 1965–1990*. Raymond: Hinds Community College [MS].

Weingarten, S., Chairman. 1965. *English in the Two-Year College*. Report of a Joint Committee of the National Council of Teachers of English and the Conference on College Composition and Communication. Champaign: NCTE.

Worthen, R. 1967. *Junior College English: Which Way?* Distributed by the National Council of Teachers of English for Members of the NCTE/CCCC Regional Conferences on English in the Two-Year College, Dec.

# 12

## Graduate Programs for Two-Year-College Faculty: History and Future Directions

### Ellen Andrews Knodt

## Introduction

As even public higher education grows more costly for students to afford and more difficult for states to fund, controversy continues to swirl around the issues of graduate education and the relative roles played by research and teaching in colleges and universities. Politicians in state legislatures, parents of undergraduates, and undergraduate students themselves often express the belief that faculty members should concentrate on teaching students and not spend as much time on research. Some faculty members at research universities and at many four-year colleges express their frustration at tenure and promotion policies that reward research, particularly publication, at the expense of undergraduate teaching. On the other hand, institutions and faculty members alike cite the need for faculty to continue to stay current in their fields and produce evidence of their expertise through published articles and books or other objective measures of their knowledge.

This controversy over the relative weight and merits of research versus teaching has many implications. First, because elite research universities put so much emphasis on research, an institution whose mission is teaching is not accorded the same status, or to put the nicest cast on it, is "second best," as L. Steven Zwerling says. Because community colleges view teaching as their primary mission, they are almost by definition accorded this inferior status by many in the academy. A second implication follows from the first and provides the issue that I examine here. Because all future college faculty (community college, four-year undergraduate college, and university alike) are trained in graduate programs at institutions that are predominantly research universities, these faculty members are likely to be trained to be researchers first and teachers second. I will look at issues surrounding graduate education for community-college faculty in the past and at attempts that have been made and are being made to devise graduate programs that may prepare faculty members better to serve the missions of the institutions in which they are employed.

## Background of Graduate Education for Two-Year-College Faculty

While issues concerning graduate programs are receiving much attention currently, we should not ignore the efforts that have been made in the last thirty years to assess and improve graduate education for two-year-college teachers. Since the dramatic increase in the development of community and junior colleges began in the 1960s, there have been and continue to be attempts to provide guidelines and programs for the education of two-year-college faculty. The master's degree continues to be the entry-level degree for community-college faculty. In perhaps the earliest assessment of two-year-college English faculty, a joint committee of NCTE and CCCC reported in 1965 that "the Master's degree is the minimum stated academic requirement for teachers in the majority [84%] of the two-year colleges participating in this study" (14). In 1969, *The Focus Report on the National Study of English in the Junior College*, an ERIC report by Richard J. Worthen and Michael F. Shugrue, pointed out that a traditional M.A. inadequately meets faculty needs because the degree is "a step toward a traditional Ph.D." (quoted in *CCCC* 305) with an emphasis on literature and literary criticism. In their study of 3,000 faculty from 263 junior colleges, Worthen and Shugrue reported that faculty acknowledge the need for more instruction in the following areas:

Techniques in teaching composition

Variety in teaching techniques

Definition and measurement of relevant course objectives

Breadth in related academic areas such as history, sociology, political science, philosophy

Knowledge of how to teach reading as a basic skill

Background in psychology and learning theory (quoted in *CCCC* 304).

This early study shows the need for breadth of subject matter, attention to teaching techniques, and focus on the primary business of the two-year-college English teacher: reading and writing. In 1971, the CCCC Executive Committee published *Guidelines for Junior College English Teacher Training Programs*, which strongly emphasized the unique nature of the junior or community college in American higher education and urged that faculty hired to teach in such institutions be given appropriate training:

> Junior college English teachers are called upon to fill new roles; they must go outside the traditional methods of teaching composition and literature in order to make literature accessible, and effective writing possible, for a much wider spectrum of the population than has ever before attended college. (303)

Following this report, a number of programs began to address the unique needs of two-year institutions. In 1977, Greg Cowan edited a CCCC report, *An Annotated List of Training Programs for Community College Teachers*, which listed forty-five colleges or universities that offered either a master's or doctor's degree designed for teachers on two-year campuses. Of these, ten institutions offered a doctoral degree (three were Ph.D.s, one was an Ed.D., and six were Doctor of Arts degrees). Several schools in California had certificate programs leading to the California Community College Credential.

Perhaps the most significant development in graduate education for two-year-college faculty was the development of a doctoral degree specifically designed as a teaching degree for faculty teaching undergraduates: the Doctor of Arts. The history of the Doctor of Arts degree and its status now, more than thirty years after inception, provide some insight into how faculty are educated for their teaching positions.

The Doctor of Arts degree, according to Judith Glazer,

> [. . .] originated at Carnegie-Mellon University [. . .] and was perceived as a major innovation that could reform the doctorate by changing its focus from the development of research scholars to the preparation of college teachers. It gained generous financial support from the Carnegie Corporation and vigorous endorsements from the Carnegie Commission on Higher Education under the leadership of Clark Kerr, who predicted that it would become "the standard degree for college teaching in the United States, a non-research degree of high prestige." (quoted in Glazer 15)

As summarized by Barton Pulling,

> The degree would develop the skills of people interested in teaching at the undergraduate level. Practical teaching experience, pedagogy, and a project or dissertation linking teaching with a discipline were and are substituted for acquiring extensive research skills and presenting a "new knowledge" dissertation. (23)

A specially designed Carnegie Mellon program for faculty currently teaching English in two-year colleges began in 1975 under the direction of Professor Jan Cohn, Director of Graduate Studies in English, who reported in a 1998 interview that the impetus for the Doctor of Arts programs came from a "reform movement" to promote "graduate education that took seriously the training of teachers [in which] research skills remained significant but were not seen as the sole purpose of graduate study." (A concurrent program also began at Carnegie Mellon for two-year-college history teachers in 1975.) By the spring of 1990, fifty-seven students had graduated from either the original Carnegie Mellon D.A. English program or the special program for two-year-college faculty (Glazer 21), including this writer and the two editors of this volume. The Carnegie Mellon D.A. was phased out in favor of a Ph.D. in rhetoric when rhetorical study achieved national prominence in the 1980s.

One of the unique features of the special Carnegie Mellon D.A. program and a major advantage for virtually all of its participants was the way that it accommodated two-year-college faculty who wished to earn a doctorate while remaining on the faculty at their institutions. That special program had two phases: the first phase required coursework in composition theory and pedagogy, reading pedagogy, and literary criticism, spaced over a period of three summers in residence at the University and one semester of a directed curriculum internship completed at the participants' home institutions. The internship included a substantial paper. Successful completion of the first phase led to the Certificate of Specialization in the Teaching of English in Two-Year Colleges. If participants wished to complete the Doctor of Arts degree, they were invited to apply for candidacy and complete phase two: (1) a substantial reading course in a literary period with several written papers completed as independent study; (2) an oral examination conducted by three members of the department covering literature and the teaching of literature (on the literary period represented by the reading course) and composition and the teaching of composition; (3) a curricular or critical scholarly dissertation; and (4) a successful oral defense of the dissertation.

Participants, who were required to have two years' experience as two-year-college teachers and hold the master's degree, were able to complete the coursework for the program over three summers while remaining as full-time faculty during the academic year. Because most two-year colleges do not allow sabbaticals or leaves of absence (see Knodt), arranging the required course work in this way met the participants' needs. Based on my informal conversations with those who completed Carnegie Mellon's degree, graduates of the program seem pleased with their experience, the preparation they received for teaching the students in their institutions, and the way Carnegie Mellon prepared them to think of themselves as leaders in their colleges and in the profession, including encouragement to publish and present conference papers. Judith Glazer reports that her 1991 survey of 350 graduates of D.A. programs nationwide found both high employment and general satisfaction among recipients of the degree: "The D.A. has by and large proved useful to its graduates, meeting their goals as practical programs that combine subject matter content and pedagogical skills, and that enable them to secure professional credentials and enhance their teaching careers"(23).

Another Doctor of Arts program of importance bears analysis because its history and its subsequent evolution into a Ph.D. program reveals much about the possibilities of graduate education. James Berlin reports the history of the graduate English program at the State University of New York at Albany in his last book *Rhetorics, Poetics, and Cultures: Refiguring College English Studies*. SUNY-Albany had its traditional literary Ph.D. program "de-registered by the state in response to financial exigencies in 1975" (157). In response, the University concentrated its graduate programs in the Doctor of Arts degree, emphasizing "pedagogy and [. . .] creative writing and rhetoric and composition" (158). As the program evolved and "developed a national reputation for producing students with strong credentials in writing and teaching" (158), more emphasis was given to the "intersection of literary theory and pedagogy"(158). Other institutions began to blend the studies of writing, teaching, and literary criticism in their English Ph.D. programs so that in 1987 the SUNY-Albany faculty "concluded that the attention to integrating pedagogy in graduate work in English had become so common in other programs that it was time to reconsider the Doctor of Arts program" (158). SUNY-Albany received approval by the state for the Ph.D. in Writing, Teaching, and Criticism in 1992 (158; see also North). Berlin sees the SUNY program as exemplary, combining pedagogy in all areas, requiring both a practicum in teaching and an internship, and emphasizing the idea that "writing, rhetoric, criticism, pedagogy, language study, and literary history constantly intersect" (158; see also North). What interests me in this discussion of the program is that SUNY-Albany felt it desirable to reestablish the Ph.D. degree even though the Doctor of Arts achieved high recognition. Though both the Carnegie Mellon and SUNY-Albany Doctor of Arts programs were successful, both institutions chose to institute Ph.D. programs, however different from the traditional literary specialist Ph.D. programs they might be. This history again suggests the power and status of the Ph.D. and suggests that we need to look for the possibility of reform in graduate English education within Ph.D. programs, rather than expecting a new kind of degree to take hold.

Notwithstanding these two examples, the Doctor of Arts has not disappeared. It is still offered at twenty-three universities in forty different disciplines, and "more than 1,900 degrees have been granted in the DA's twenty-one year existence" (Pulling 23). However, the degree has not fulfilled Clark Kerr's expectations of becoming the major degree for college teaching, and most authorities do not now think it will. Glazer's conclusion notes that the reason the D.A. has had a minimal impact on graduate education is that graduate faculty and deans intent on protecting the status and prestige of their institutions as doctorate-granting research institutions are not about to elevate teaching over research and, therefore, are unlikely to promote a teaching degree that is an alternative to the research-oriented Ph.D. (24). She says that when "change agents" such as the Carnegie Corporation or state boards withdrew support for the D.A., the D.A. programs lost their "academic legitimacy within the education establishment"(24). Reasons for the withdrawal of support from foundations and state agencies vary, according to Glazer, from the reclassification of some institutions from Comprehensive Doctorate Granting to Research 1 and 2, to states' attempts to limit duplicative graduate degrees, to changes in the academic labor market (22–23). The fact that community colleges employ almost twice as many adjuncts as full-time faculty (as reported below) may account for a decline in demand for the D.A., because adjuncts have few incentives and no financial support to enter doctoral programs. Whatever the causes of degree discontinuance, the perceived lack of "academic legitimacy" of the D.A., reported by D.A. graduates in Glazer's survey as "the negative reaction of colleagues toward the D.A. degree"(23), was the one major disappointment among such graduates. Glazer's conclusion reminds us of the continuing controversy over research and teaching: "In the final analysis, the experiences of those involved in DA programs document the continuing dichotomy between individuals who do research and individuals who teach, a dichotomy that remains to be bridged on both the theoretical and practical levels"(24).

## Future Direction of Graduate Education for Two-Year-College Faculty

If graduate education is to meet the needs of faculty teaching in two-year colleges and in four-year colleges with a primary teaching mission, pressures from outside the research universities will need to be the "change agents," as Glazer puts it. As surprising as it may seem, such "change agents" may be the two-year colleges themselves. Even though two-year colleges do not enjoy high status in the academic community, they could play an important role in determining appropriate graduate training for their faculty because of their sheer economic weight: The American Asso-

ciation of Community Colleges reports that "community college students represent 53% of the public undergraduate population in 1992" (5)
and community colleges employ 100,000 full-time and 190,000 part-
time faculty (73). A statement by the Conference on Growing Use of
Part-Time and Adjunct Faculty in the January/February 1998 issue of
*Academe* underscores the growing importance of community colleges
in American higher education: "The community college share of all
higher education faculty appointments increased from 19 percent in 1970
to 32 percent in 1993" (54–55). If graduate schools at the nation's
research universities wish to place their graduates in teaching jobs (and
thereby attract more graduate students to their programs), they would be
advised to acknowledge that their graduates may find themselves teaching in two-year institutions and be more willing to prepare their graduate students for such teaching. If community colleges would lobby as a
group for more teaching-centered preparation in graduate courses and
also hire graduates of programs who had the appropriate preparation,
then graduate schools might be motivated to change. That being said,
however, the most selective graduate schools, which aim to prepare their
students for positions in research universities similar to themselves and
have no interest in preparing students to teach in two-year colleges, would
be resistant to any change in the graduate programs. Many Ph.D. candidates report being actively discouraged by graduate-school advisors from
seeking positions at even those four-year colleges where teaching is a
primary mission, and two-year colleges are considerably farther down
the list.

Even though research universities seem reluctant to give more
emphasis to teaching in preparing their graduate students, many leading
educators representing such elite institutions have been calling for reform
in the nature of graduate training for college teachers, especially in doctoral programs. Peter Brooks in a 1996 article in *The Chronicle of Higher
Education* notes the number of recent books and articles, including
Bowen and Rudenstines's *In Pursuit of the Ph.D.* (1991) and Menand's
*New York Times Magazine* article (1996) calling for a streamlining of
the Ph.D. process or an elimination of the doctoral dissertation in order
to speed a candidate's progress to the degree. Brooks suggests instead
that graduate education should include more "apprenticeship" roles for
graduate students:

> What if one were to break the mold of the classroom, at least part of
> the time, and try to replicate the model of the aspiring biologist work-
> ing in the lab under the direction of his or her professor? Instead of sim-
> ply taking courses, students might coauthor essays with their professors,
> a form of collaboration common in the sciences. As well as working as
> teaching assistants for existing courses, students might, together with

their teachers, plan, research, and choose books for a course in a given subject. Whether or not the course is ever taught, the experience could teach more about conceptualizing and transmitting a subject than would taking another graduate seminar. (A52)

Such "apprenticeships" would place a greater emphasis on the real-world activities of a faculty member teaching undergraduates and prepare graduate students for their duties in most four-year and two-year-college classes.

Further criticism of the present system of graduate education comes from Robert H. Atwell, president emeritus of the American Council on Education, who says that American higher education suffers from a "single model of excellence" in which producing Ph.D.s to do research is the only goal for a quality institution. This single model is "out of touch with the needs of the nation and with the academic marketplace. What we and the nation need are multiple models of excellence, reflecting different but equally worthy educational missions." Atwell discusses several multiple models, specifically citing the contributions of community colleges: "Community colleges are at the leading edge in work-force training, the use of educational technology, and flexibility in responding to changing student needs. As a group, they are America's most exciting colleges." He suggests that many four-year colleges have the potential to realize their own model of excellence:

> Regional state colleges and universities share many of the same virtues as community colleges in terms of their emphasis on teaching and service, but, unfortunately, too many of them aspire to become research institutions offering doctoral degrees. They have significant numbers of young faculty members who resent the teaching loads they carry and are unsympathetic to the "underprepared" students they teach.

The dichotomy of research vs. teaching and its attendant status issues prevent institutions from realizing their missions and produce frustration in faculty members.

Atwell has several practical suggestions for improving graduate training: (1) Give graduating seniors interested in graduate school a more realistic idea of the job market; (2) Require all Ph.D. students to know the diversity of educational institutions and what each type wants from faculty members; (3) Require supervised teaching of all graduate students who teach or wish to teach undergraduates, including "classroom visits by senior professors, videotaping of lectures, and seminars addressing pedagogical questions"; (4) Increase the breadth of formal study during Ph.D. programs and reduce the amount of time devoted to dissertation research; and (5) Inform graduate faculty about what experiences and training colleges want in their newly hired faculty members.

If Atwell's suggestions were followed, graduate students would have a wider choice of job possibilities and be better prepared to succeed at an institution whose primary mission is teaching. Graduate schools would offer graduate students a choice in taking a greater breadth of subjects or in specializing more narrowly. Teaching skills would improve because of an increased focus on pedagogy. Finally, the whole enterprise of higher education would benefit from cooperation among the various types of institutions. Four-year colleges and universities can ill afford to ignore what goes on educationally in community colleges because they get many of their upper-division students from such institutions: According to the *Community College Fact Book*, in 1985, "Forty percent of the students who completed their two-year degrees at a two-year college entered a four-year institution" (26). With the inauguration of the Hope Scholarships in 1998, providing tax incentives for students to attend college for at least two years, the demand for community-college faculty will likely increase and the need for appropriate graduate education will become even more acute.

## Suggested Ways to Accomplish Change in Graduate English Programs

If we acknowledge the difficulty of changing the culture of research institutions to accept an alternative to the Ph.D. degree, perhaps those of us active in community-college administration as department or division chairs who hire new faculty or as representatives to organizations of two-year-college faculty could establish communication with graduate-school deans and placement offices to lobby for the kinds of courses and experiences that would prepare new community-college faculty within existing M.A. and Ph.D. programs. Graduate-program directors, moreover, should be receptive to designing programs in consultation with experienced two-year-college teachers, whom they should seek out for advice and counsel on the appropriate graduate work for teaching English in two-year institutions. Robert Atwell's suggestions could also be implemented within existing programs. State legislatures and boards of education can be informed about the need to make changes in graduate education to prepare community-college faculty. Articles in journals or speeches at conferences addressing the need for changes within existing programs may help create a climate that will foster change. Several recent articles suggest that some collaborations among universities and two-year colleges for improved two-year faculty preparation are beginning to occur (see Elder et al.; Buck and Frank; Cowan, Traver, and Riddle; Murphy; and Salmon). The 2003 Preparing Future Faculties (PFF) report of the ten-year initiative of the Council of Graduate Schools and the

Association of American Colleges and Universities also offers hope for more effective collaboration among four-year and two-year institutions (see *PFF Web*).

The following excerpt from a conference presentation illustrates one such approach. In an address to a Speech Communication Association conference in July 1996 entitled "Are Graduate Schools Serving Community Colleges?", Isa N. Engelberg listed the qualifications that hiring committees consider in applicants for community-college faculty positions in addition to a master's degree:

1. Extent of relevant teaching experience
2. Extent of educational preparation in areas related to anticipated course assignments
3. Extent of experience in, or potential for working effectively with, a diverse multiethnic student population
4. Extent of scope and diversity of content areas in which teaching assignments can be undertaken
5. Extent of willingness to cooperate with colleagues and peers in developing and implementing departmental philosophy and objectives
6. Extent of professional background and experience
7. Extent of ability to contribute to cocurricular programs
8. Extent of ability to teach specific, basic courses.

If community-college faculty and administrators, more secure now in their positions in higher education after their long "track record," would make known the qualities desired in new faculty members and cultivate those qualities in their existing faculty through encouraging professional development, community colleges would become an even more effective part of higher education in this country. Community colleges have had their infancy and adolescence and are poised now to move into the most fruitful period of their adult maturity.

## Works Cited

American Association of Community Colleges. 1995. *National Profile of Community Colleges: Trends and Statistics. 1995–1996.* Washington: Amer. Assoc. of Community Colleges.

*An Annotated List of Training Programs for Community College English Teachers: A CCCC Report.* 1977. Edited by Greg Cowan. ERIC Clearinghouse on Reading and Communication Skills (March).

Atwell, R. H. 1996. "Doctoral Education Must Match Needs and Realities." *The Chronicle of Higher Education* 29 (Nov): B4.

Berlin, J. A. 1996. *Rhetorics, Poetics, and Cultures: Refiguring College English Studies*. Urbana: NCTE.

Bowen, W. G., and N. Rudenstine. 1991. *In Pursuit of the Ph.D.* Princeton: Princeton UP.

Brooks, P. 1996. "Graduate Learning As Apprenticeship." *The Chronicle of Higher Education* 20 (Dec.): A52.

Buck, J., and MacGregor F. 2001. "Preparing Future Faculty: A Faculty-in-Training Program." *Teaching English in the Two-Year College* 28: 241–50.

CCCC Executive Committee. 1971. "Guidelines for Junior College English Teacher Training Programs." *College Composition and Communication* 22: 303–13.

Cohn, J. 1998. Personal interview. 16 Jan.

Cowan, T., J. Traver, and T. H. Riddle. 2001. "A TA Perspective of a Community College Faculty-in-Training Pilot Program." *Teaching English in the Two-Year College* 28: 251–58.

Elder, D., et al. 1997. "Community Colleges Train the Professoriate of the Future." *Teaching English in the Two-Year College* 24: 118–25.

Engelberg, I. N. 1996. Address to Speech Communication Association Summer Conference on Graduate Education in Communication. Washington, D.C. July 19.

*English in the Two-Year College: Report of a Joint Committee of NCTE and CCCC*. 1965. Champaign: NCTE.

Gaff, J. G., et al. 2003. *Preparing Future Faculty in the Humanities and Social Sciences*. Washington, D.C.: Council of Graduate Schools.

Glazer, J. S. 1993. "The Doctor of Arts: Retrospect and Prospect." *New Directions in Teaching: Preparing Faculty for the New Conceptions in Scholarship*. San Francisco: Jossey. 15–25.

Knodt, E. 1988. "Taming Hydra: The Problem of Balancing Teaching and Scholarship at a Two-Year College." *Teaching English in the Two-Year College* 15: 170–75.

Menand, L. 1996. "How to Make a Ph.D. Matter." *New York Times Magazine* 22 (Sept.): 78.

Murphy, S. P. 2001. "Improving Two-Year College Teacher Preparation: Graduate Student Internships." *Teaching English in the Two-Year College* 28: 259–64.

North, S. M. 2000. *Refiguring the Ph.D. in English Studies: Writing, Doctoral Education, and the Fusion-Based Curriculum*. Urbana: NCTE.

*PFF Web*. 2003. <www.preparing-faculty.org>.

Pulling, B. S. 1992. "More on the (Ir)relevant Ph.D. The D.A., Alive in Idaho." *Academe* 78.5: 23.

Salmon, V. N. 2001. "The National Center for Community College Education:

A Doctoral Program with Difference. *Teaching English in the Two-Year College* 28: 265–70.

"Statement from the Conference on the Growing Use of Part-Time and Adjunct Faculty." 1998. *Academe* 84.1: 54–60.

Zwerling, L. S. 1976. *Second Best.* New York: McGraw.

# 13

## Teaching English in Two-Year Colleges: A Review of Selected Studies

### Howard Tinberg

"What does a plumber need with Chaucer?"
—a dean quoted in McPherson 141

To responsibly teach the "new student" is not to water down traditional approaches; it is to do something different.
—Gibson ix

## The Promise and the Problem

A conversation that I once had with a nursing colleague at my two-year college conveys for me the contradictory nature of two-year-college teaching at the beginning of this new century. There we were in the college's writing lab, chatting about the work that we were truly excited about: meeting students where they were, promoting a critical self-awareness in the students who came to the lab for help. But then came the question. My colleague wondered whether the work that I was doing was enough to satisfy my obvious "intellectual curiosity." I took no offense at what she asked, nor do I respect her less for asking it. But I couldn't help wondering why teaching at the community college could become equated with work that calls for so little intellectual engagement. Why must being a community-college teacher not satisfy such intellectual needs? Why can't it enjoy the privileged status of work elsewhere in higher education (see Reynolds "The Intellectual")?

That our conversation was taking place in a writing lab brings to mind the important role of two-year colleges in pioneering writing and tutoring centers and of establishing innovative strategies for assessing and monitoring student work. Moreover, that two colleagues from such different disciplines (I from English and my friend from nursing) could in fact be comfortable talking about our work testifies to our status as "expert generalists," with little vested interest in academic territory (unlike colleagues at universities, where hyperspecialization is still the rule rather than the exception) (Reynolds, "Twenty-Five" 233). We are far more accustomed to crossing borders than our four-year counterparts, given our commitment to the comprehensive mission of the two-year college and to the importance of teaching (Tinberg). Why shouldn't a teacher of writing and literature speak to a teacher of nursing (who is also a practicing nurse)?

But my colleague's concern points to a central motif in the two-year-college narrative, namely the ambivalent and ambiguous role occupied by the community college in the academy (Brint and Karabel; Dougherty). In an influential report on two-year-college English known as the Tempe Report (the record of a conference that took place in 1965 at Arizona State University cosponsored by ASU, the National Council of Teachers of English, and the Conference on College Composition and Communication) Albert R. Kitzhaber began by stating the obvious:

> The two-year college, as we all know, occupies an uneasy position between the high school and the four-year college, and sometimes appears to be so dominated by the one or the other that it loses a clear identity of its own. (Archer 3)

Usually, the dilemma is stated baldly and reductively: Are community colleges an extension of the high schools into grades 13 and 14 or do they reproduce the lower-division curriculum of the four-year colleges? Histories of the two-year-college movement suggest a split early on between such visions of the "junior college." Some, like University of Michigan president Henry Tappan, saw the junior college as a German-style gymnasium, where students would take college preparatory courses, leaving universities to teach the more privileged, upper-level university courses (Zwerling 44). (It is interesting to note recent actions on the part of universities to cede the teaching of developmental courses to community colleges in the light of such a history. For more on the subject of the "remediation wars," see Tinberg "An Interview.") And yet other influential scholars called for a kind of second-tier college but a college nonetheless—William Rainey Harper, president of the University of Chicago, actually created a "junior college" within the university (Zwerling 46). Movement away from this rather simplistic view of what two-year colleges can offer toward a more comprehensive mission had to await the passage of the federal Vocation Education Act of 1963 and the tremendous explosion of two-year colleges very quickly thereafter (Cohen and Brawer, *The American* 198).

# If They Build Them, Who Shall Teach?

Kitzhaber's comments reflect a concern felt by many in higher education just as the community-college explosion began in the 1960s: the need to define their mission and to prepare a generation of teachers to meet the challenge posed by that mission. Within English studies itself, a whole slew of reports appeared at about this time to consider the problem of devising a curriculum and initiating appropriate teacher preparation, beginning with the NCTE/CCCC study *English in the Two-Year College* (Weingarten and Kroger). Reporting on a survey of 239 two-year colleges, Weingarten and Kroeger paint a picture that is pretty much still with us: Faculty are overworked, their classes are overenrolled, and they are given few opportunities for professional development (Weingarten 16, 74). Shortly thereafter *Research and the Development of English Programs in the Junior College* (the Tempe Report mentioned earlier) was published (Archer). In that study, representatives of four- and two-year colleges attempt to identify six key areas for consideration: teacher preparation and in-service training, junior college and high school articulation, two- and four-year college connections, community and continuing education, teaching English to transfer students, and teaching English to so-called "terminal students" (Archer iii). Clearly, it would no longer do to see the two-year college as reproducing the first two years of the college English curriculum, given the diversity of students coming through the open doors of community colleges. Nor would it suffice to see the two-year college as merely an extension of high school because so many two-year-college students would be transferring to four-year institutions. It is perhaps the most astonishing revelation of all about the two-year college that some at the conference viewed the two-year-college teacher of English as more than merely teaching English. Faculty imbibe and express the democratic principles of open admission and universal opportunity (Archer 32). That notion had, and continues to have, a dramatic effect on the way two-year-college faculty view themselves and the work that they do.

Taking up a key theme from these earlier studies, Michael Shugrue's report on the *National Study of English in the Junior College*, sponsored by the Modern Language Association, the ERIC Clearinghouse on the Teaching of English in Higher Education, and the National Council of Teachers of English recommends continuous and significant faculty development for teachers already employed at the two-year college, as well as preservice training for those interested in joining the faculty (Shugrue). *The Guidelines for Junior College English Teacher Training Programs*, whose development was authorized by the CCCC Executive Committee, list some twenty-one "necessary competencies," beginning with "recognize and respect the wide range of backgrounds, abilities, interests, and career goals of junior college students" (Cowan 305). Other competencies reflect the profession's commitment to whole language instruction and preserving students' rights to respect for their own languages and dialects (305). Every teacher training program ought to include study in the following areas: linguistics, literature, rhetoric, teaching skill, writing, reading, speaking, related disciplines, training in evaluating student work, interning, and electives (Cowan 306–10).

A number of problems arise in trying to implement such training, as Keats Sparrow and Bertie Fearing have shown. The first problem is the difficulty of implementing a program that attempts to meet the various competencies needed to teach at the two-year college. An additional problem, according to Sparrow and Fearing, is determining who should staff such programs. Specialists in universities may indeed have an expertise in the field of teacher training but may be unwilling or unable to cover the practical needs of two-year-college teachers and students. If veteran two-year-college instructors are hired to join such university programs, the lack of a terminal degree creates problems for credibility and tenure, according to Sparrow and Fearing. In addition, continuing misperceptions among graduate programs about two-year-college work hinder their ability to attract quality students into their programs (that there is little difference between two- and four-year college teaching, for example). Evidence abounds that graduate programs have failed to provide adequate teaching preparation for work in the two-year college (Kroll 201).

A more recent and, perhaps, more compelling challenge facing community colleges is their increasing reliance on part-time or contingent faculty. Most instruction at the community college is performed by contingent faculty. Indeed, a survey taken in the previous decade indicated that sixty-six percent of all community college faculty were part-time (as quoted in Worthen 42). How will such staffing affect the historic mission of the comprehensive community college? Will faculty continue to provide both individualized instruction and service to the college (including advisement and committee work) and respond, as well, to community needs?

## "Disciplining" Open Admissions

Historically, the question of what two-year-college English faculty were teaching was shaped inevitably by open admissions itself, the defining characteristic of the two-year college. "Democracy's Open Door," as the community college has been called, is open to those who in generations past would never have experienced higher education (Griffith and Connor). What exactly would faculty in English teach these students? How was the discipline of English itself altered by the presence of these students? Teacher narratives from those early days of open admissions in the 1960s are remarkable resources for understanding the phenomenon. Each tries to describe what it was like to teach the "new student" (that is, the underprepared student), fascinating us to this day with their mix of exhilaration, missionary zeal, and exasperation at the hugeness of the task that lay before these teachers.

Commenting on the behavior of teachers when presented on that first day with the challenge of instructing basic writers, Mina Shaughnessy, who directed the basic writing program at City College of the City University of New York during its open admissions experiment, observed the following:

> Sensing no need to relate what he is teaching to what his students know, to stop to explore the contexts within which the conventions of academic discourse have developed, and to view these conventions in patterns large enough to encompass what students do know about language already, the teacher becomes a mechanic of the sentence, the paragraph, and the essay. (Shaughnessy 290–91)

Inevitably, as Shaughnessy notes, such a teacher must confront the reality on the ground: The writing problems presented by these open admissions students simply would not abide containment within neat categories, nor could they be resolved through sentence grammar exercises. The teacher needed to "dive in" and study the errors that characterized these students' pages. Adrienne Rich, who taught alongside Mina Shaughnessy in the SEEK program at City College for disadvantaged youths, taught reading and writing in ways that spoke to students directly. "We were dealing," she writes, "not simply with dialect and syntax but with the imagery of lives, the anger and flame of urban youth—how could this be *used*?" (56). For these students, it simply wouldn't be business as usual. That is, it would not suffice to write the usual themes (perhaps in response to standardized readers) or to engage in the conventions of parsing a line of verse. Faculty had to meet the students "where they lived," as the saying in those days went.

These new students daily forced English teachers to ask, "What is this class for?" (McPherson 45). It was, and continues to be, a dangerous question for English teachers to ask, especially in the two-year college. Given its apparent call for utility in English studies, many might very well view it, as one two-year college-teacher notes derisively, as "spelling for secretaries" or as calling into question the very role of humanities at the two-year college (Scally 72).

That same teacher, arguing that a purely utilitarian model for writing instruction leads only to frustration for all, sees the teaching of writing as an opportunity to map out "moral growth" (72). Certainly the process movement of the 1960s and 1970s found an agreeable audience in two-year-college faculty, eager as we have been to work from students' own experiences rather than a prescribed set of preestablished texts. This is not to say that the two-year-college writing classroom might not serve a useful role in teaching workplace writing, especially technical writing. Nell Ann Picket, a pioneering presence in technical writing in the two-year college, has argued compellingly for the justness of such a role and for the fitness of the faculty to play it (Pickett).

The survival of writing courses at the community college has never been questioned, given the assumed importance outside the academy of writing and reading skills. More contentious has been the place of literature instruction within the two-year college, or, more profoundly, the place of the humanities themselves (Yarrington). How does humanities instruction fit with career and developmental programs? Judith Rae Davis and Sandra Silverberg, both of Bergen Community College in New Jersey, have written about an attempt at their own college to reconfigure the disciplines, including the humanities, in a program called The Integration Project. Drawing on recent scholarship in gender, race, ethnicity, and class, the college has sought to bridge a variety of disciplines through themes that such scholarship provides. As such, it plays powerfully to one of the strengths of community college teaching—the generalist nature of that teaching and the willingness of faculty to cross disciplinary borders. Ultimately, the task of the two-year-college teacher of English might lie well beyond providing expertise in English per se. "The successful college teacher of the future," writes James E. Russell,

> will be more concerned with how students integrate the curriculum than with how the scholars do it. He will look to each student, ask what has been the pattern of his intellectual activity, and plan the next steps accordingly. He will strive to help the student discover the relationships of new study to earlier knowledge; he will challenge him to bring to a problem many insights from many sources; and he will evaluate his success not only in terms of mastery of discipline, but also in terms of his progress in understanding relationships. (quoted in Barton 14)

The community colleges seem poised to play such an integrative role and the discipline of English might very well be a key site for that kind of work. And yet two-year-college English may provide the setting for an altogether different kind of work. Rather than integrative, it may serve a more mediatory role; rather than derivative, it may strike out in a far more original direction. Two-year-college English may fashion its own kind of scholarship and research.

# Fashioning a New Kind of Scholarship and Research

Any bibliographic work on the two-year college must confront a central irony: that most of the scholarship and research about the community college has traditionally been done by those not teaching in the two-year-college classroom. Certainly a great deal of research has been done on the community-college movement, especially since the boom of the 1960s. Foundational works such as Arthur Cohen and Florence Brawer's *The American Community College; The Collegiate Function of Community Colleges*; their edited series of monographs, Jossey-Bass' New Directions for Community Colleges; and K. Patricia Cross' *Beyond the Open Door: New Students in Higher Education* have been especially useful in telling the history of two-year colleges and in positioning the community college within the context of higher education generally. But detailed, ethnographically rich discussions of what actually takes place within the two-year-college classroom are still rare things. (Howard London's published dissertation *The Culture of a Community College* did break important ground in that respect; Griffith and Connor, former two-year-college English teachers, do provide significant insights and suggest the importance of two-year professionals telling their stories; and, more recently, W. Norton Grubb and associates have produced an "inside look" at community-college teaching.) Scholarship and research on teaching English in the two-year college are represented essentially in the NCTE journal *Teaching English in the Two-Year College* (*TETYC*) and in an important collection of essays edited by Mark Reynolds, *Two-Year College English: Essays for a New Century*. Although skewed by its authors' critical agenda, Dennis McGrath and Martin Spear's *The Academic Crisis of the Community College* does offer a useful critique of writing-across-the-curriculum as practiced within the two-year college. Also noteworthy is the recent collection of essays, *The Politics of Writing in the Two-Year College*, edited by Barry Alford and Keith Kroll, which takes a critical look at writing instruction in two-year institutions.

The challenge for two-year-college teachers of English (and their colleagues elsewhere in the curriculum) is to see themselves as knowledge makers (see Reynolds "Two-Year College Teachers" and Tinberg *Border-Talk*). Ernest Boyer's call for recognition in the academy of a "scholarship of teaching" and Thomas Angelo and K. Patricia Cross' advocacy of classroom research have, without a doubt, direct implications for two-year-college faculty (Boyer 23; Angelo and Cross). If recognition for such work is granted, two-year-college faculty will gain a certain measure of prestige. But, as I have argued elsewhere, such calls may have the overall effect of increasing the separation between what two-year-college faculty do and the more privileged form of research and scholarship that university professors engage in (Tinberg, *Border-Talk* viii).

Instead, two-year-college teachers of English may find it far more exhilarating and far more productive to see themselves enacting what Henry Giroux calls a "border pedagogy," to teach along the borders of specialized disciplines and communities (28). Perhaps two-year-college faculty will one day have a hand in reconceptualizing the very notion of what a community might consist of. "The age of the professor is over," write two youthful community-college teachers about the impact of information technology on what it is teachers do,

> No longer will teachers be the repositories of knowledge and dictators of truth—but they will become guides who act as explorers with their students of the electronic knowledge bases open to everyone. One's knowledge will no longer be judged by what one can remember, but on how well one can navigate [. . .] . The information network, if uncorrupted by those who wish to protect the knowledge hoard of the select few, will become the truly democratic university of tomorrow, providing information and power to all: a community college for the world community. (Harris and Hooks 161)

Even as community colleges lead the way toward such broad-based change in learning, they will continue to display a commitment to individualized instruction. With the use of technology, Mark Reynolds reminds us, community-college teachers will continue to "adjust teaching to individual learning styles" ("The Past and Future" 318).

The language, the tone—all seem familiar, recalling the mission, the zeal (and perhaps a bit of the excessive pride) of those who entered the two-year-college profession during the rush of the 1960s. This much is surely true: The work of teaching English in the two-year college looks to be just as exciting in the first decades of the twenty-first century as it has been in the last thirty years. And that is saying something.

# Works Cited

Alford, B., and K. Kroll, eds. 2001. *The Politics of Writing in the Two-Year College*. Westport: Boynton.

Angelo, T. A., and K. P. Cross. 1993. *Classroom Assessment Techniques: A Handbook for College Teachers*. San Francisco: Jossey.

Archer, J. W., and W. A. Ferrell. 1965. *Research and the Development of English Programs in the Junior College: Proceedings of the Tempe Conference*. Champaign: NCTE.

Barton, T. L., and A. M. Beachner. 1970. *Teaching English in the Two-Year College*. Menlo Park: Cummings.

Boyer, E. L. 1990. *Scholarship Reconsidered: Priorities of the Professoriate*. Princeton: Carnegie Foundation for the Advancement of Teaching.

Brint, S., and J. Karabel. 1989. *The Diverted Dream*. New York: Oxford UP.

Cohen, A. M., and F. Brawer. 1989. *The American Community College*. 2nd ed. San Francisco: Jossey.

———. 1987. *The Collegiate Function of Community Colleges*. San Francisco: Jossey.

———, ed. 1973. New Directions for Community Colleges Series. San Francisco: Jossey.

Cowan, G. 1971. "Guidelines for Junior College English Teacher Training Programs." *College Composition and Communication* 22: 303–13.

Cross, K. P. 1971. *Beyond the Open Door: New Students in Higher Education*. San Francisco: Jossey.

Davis, J. R., and S. S. Silverberg. 1994. "The Integration Project: A Model for Curriculum Transformation." In *Two-Year College English,* edited by M. Reynolds, 108–19.

Dougherty, K. J. 2001. *The Contradictory College*. Albany: State U of New York P.

Gibson, W., ed. 1979. *New Students in Two-Year Colleges: Twelve Essays*. Urbana: NCTE.

Giroux, H. 1992. *Border Crossings: Cultural Workers and the Politics of Education*. New York: Routledge.

Griffith, M., and A. Connor. 1994. *Democracy's Open Door: The Community College in America's Future*. Portsmouth: Heinemann.

Grubb, W. N. 1999. *Honored But Invisible: An Inside Look at Teaching in Community Colleges*. New York: Routledge.

Harris, M. C., and J. Hooks. 1994. "Writing in Cyber-Space: Communication, Community, and the Electronic Network." In *Two-Year College English,* edited by M. Reynolds, 151–62.

Kroll, K. 1994. "(Re)Viewing Faculty Preservice Training and Development." In *Two-Year College English,* edited by M. Reynolds, 196–211.

London, H. 1978. *The Culture of a Community College*. New York: Praeger.

McGrath D., and M. B. Spear. 1991. *The Academic Crisis of the Community College*. Albany: State U of New York.

McPherson, E. 1990. "Remembering, Regretting, and Rejoicing: The Twenty-Fifth Anniversary of the Two-Year College Regionals." *College Composition and Communication* 41: 137–50.

Pickett, N. 1990. "Teaching Technical Communication in Two-Year Colleges: The Courses and the Teachers. *The Technical Writing Teacher* 16: 76–85.

Reynolds, M. 1998. "The Intellectual Work of Two-Year College Teaching." *ADE Bulletin* (Winter): 37–40.

———. 2002. "The Past and Future of (Two-Year) College English Studies." In *The Relevance of English: Teaching That Matters in Students' Lives*, edited by R. P. Yagelski and S. A. Leonard. Urbana: National Council of Teachers of English. 307–23.

———. 1990. "Twenty-Five Years of Two-Year College English." *Teaching English in the Two-Year College* 17: 230–35.

———. ed. 1994. *Two-Year College English: Essays for a New Century*. Urbana: NCTE.

———. 2005. "Two-Year College Teachers as Knowledge Makers." This anthology.

Rich, A. 1979. "Teaching Language in Open Admissions." In *On Lies, Secrets, and Silences: Selected Prose 1966–1978*. New York: Norton. 51–68.

Scally, J. 1979. "Composition and Moral Education." In *New Students in Two-Year Colleges: Twelve Essays*, edited by Walker Gibson. Urbana: NCTE. 69–86.

Shaugnessy, M. P. 1997. "Diving In: An Introduction to Basic Writing." In *Cross-Talk in Comp Theory: A Reader*, edited by V. Villanueva, Jr. Urbana: NCTE. 289–95.

Shugrue, M. F. 1970. *The National Study of English in the Junior College*. New York: The ERIC Clearinghouse on the Teaching of English in Higher Education. ED 37 480.

Sparrow, W. K., and B. E. Fearing. 1980. "New Kid on the Block: Graduate Programs for Two-Year College English Teachers." *CEA Forum* 11: 7–12.

Tinberg, H. 1997. *Border-Talk: Writing and Knowing in the Two-Year College*. Urbana: NCTE.

———. 1999. "An Interview with Ira Shor. Part I." *Teaching English in the Two-Year College*. Special Twenty-Fifth Anniversary Edition. 27: 51–60.

Weingarten, S., and F. P. Kroeger. 1965. *English in the Two-Year College: Report of a Joint Committee of the National Council of Teachers of English and Conference on College Composition and Communication*. Champaign: NCTE.

Worthen, H. 2001. "The Problem of the Majority Contingent Faculty in the Community Colleges." In *The Politics of Writing in the Two-Year College*, edited by B. Alford and K. Kroll. Portsmouth: Heinemann. 42–60.

Yarrington, R., ed. 1980. *Strengthening Humanities in Community College*. Washington: Amer. Assoc. of Community and Junior Colleges.

Zwerling, L. S. 1976. *Second Best: The Crisis of the Community College*. New York: McGraw.

# Editors

**Mark Reynolds** chairs the humanities division and teaches English at Jefferson Davis Community College in Brewton, Alabama,. where he has spent his entire career. He has been active in two-year college professional activities at the local, state, and national levels for many years, having served on NCTE, CCCC, and MLA committees. He is the author of numerous articles on teaching composition and literature and on professional issues He edited *Two-Year College English: Essays for a New Century* (NCTE, 1994) and served for seven years as the editor of the NCTE journal *Teaching English in the Two-Year College (TETYC)*. He is currently working with Howard Tinberg on a collection of What Works for Me pieces from *TETYC*.

A college professor and administrator, writer, consultant, and business owner, **Sylvia Holladay-Hicks** holds a BS and MA from Auburn University and a Doctor of Arts in English from Carnegie Mellon University. In 1997, she retired as director of the communications program at St. Petersburg Junior College. Since then she has been teaching as an adjunct at SPJC and Hillsborough Community College, as well as writing and working in her business, Premier Auctions Inc., as a licensed auctioneer. She began teaching at SPJC in 1962 and has participated actively in the development of the new profession of teaching English in the two-year college. She has been active professionally (serving on various state, regional, and national boards and committees) and has taught every writing and literature course offered in two-year college English. She has published over 200 articles and three textbooks, including *The Bedford Guide for College Writers,* now in its seventh edition, and the upcoming textbook *Bridges: A Reader for College Writers* (Pearson/Prentice-Hall).

# Contributors

In her former life, **Dee Brock** was senior vice president for education for the Public Broadcasting Service (PBS); a college teacher and administrator in the Dallas County Community College District in Texas; and, at various times, a writer, public relations/marketing executive, and consultant. Now, she is a partner in FAQs Press, a small publishing company, and coauthor of *Food FAQs: Substitutions, Yields & Equivalents*, a kitchen reference book. She is an active advocate and volunteer for several library organizations. In addition, she is president of the League of Women Voters of Tyler and Littera, a literary club, and serves on the board of the Tyler Civic Theatre Center. She has three sons; holds a Ph.D. in English from the University of North Texas; and is an enthusiast for opera, theater, travel, cooking, and, most of all, books.

**William Costanzo** is the Nancy and William Olson Professor of English at Westchester Community College, New York, where he has taught courses in writing, literature, and cinema since 1970. Bill has been a pioneer in the national media literacy movement, seeking to integrate computers, film, television, and other media into the English curriculum. His publications include *Double Exposure: Composing through Writing and Film* (1984), *The Electronic Text: Learning to Write, Read, and Reason with Computers* (1989), *Reading the Movies* (1992), *Rereading the Movies* (2004), and *The Writer's Eye* (2005).

**Beverly Derden Fatherree** has taught at Hinds Community College in Raymond, Mississippi, since 1981. She teaches or has taught all levels of composition, American and British literature, and creative writing. A member of TYCA-SE since 1981, she has served on the Regional Executive Committee, presented numerous conference sessions on subjects as varied as Alternate Texts in Teaching, the Grotesque in Southern Literature, Lee Smith and the Family as Place, Southern Women Writers and the Civil Rights Movement, and a one-woman show on Flannery O'Connor. In addition, she is on the Editorial Board of *Teaching English in the Two-Year College*.

**Ellen Andrews Knodt** is Professor of English at Penn State Abington, formerly a two-year, now a four-year branch campus of Penn State University. She teaches writing courses and American literature, specializing in the work of Ernest Hemingway. She has written three composition textbooks and contributes articles on composition, faculty development issues, and literature to essay collections and to such journals as *TETYC*, *The Journal of Teaching Writing*, *The Hemingway Review*, and *North Dakota Quarterly*.

**Mary Sue Koeppel** taught with Roger Garrison at the National Institute for Teachers of Writing and the Master Teacher Seminar in Portland, Maine, from

1980 until his death. She teaches writing at Florida Community College at Jacksonville and is the longtime editor of *Kalliope, a Journal of Literature and Art*. Among her books are *In the Library of Silences*, *Poems of Loss*, and the college textbook *Writing Strategies Plus Collaboration*.

**Ann Laster**, Hinds Community College, Raymond, Mississippi, emerita, taught a variety of English courses over thirty-six years at HCC. Her specialty area is technical communication. She is a well-recognized author in this specialty. For twenty years Laster served on the faculty of the Institute in Technical Communication, and for sixteen of those years also served as codirector. She was an active member of NCTE, CCCC, and ATTW (Fellow), and continues her membership in TYCA-SE, an organization she has served in many leadership roles, including three terms as Chair. Laster has received numerous awards, including the TYCA-SE Cowan Award, the Mississippi College Distinguished English Alumna award, and the Mississippi Carnegie Professor of the Year award.

**Marilyn Smith Layton** has been a member of the humanities faculty at North Seattle Community College since 1969. In her many years of teaching, she has focused on writing and literature classes, and has also taught in integrated studies programs once or twice yearly. Smith has also been the advisor since 1998 of Phi Theta Kappa International Honor Society, Alpha Epsilon Omega Chapter—a chapter regionally and internationally recognized. Her work as advisor inspired her to create a course last year at North Seattle on Service Learning and Leadership. Smith has authored three books and several articles. One of her special interests is the creative process and its relationship to fear and healing; she participates in the creative process as a writer and a painter, encouraging creativity in her students through their class assignments.

**Alan Meyers** has been teaching in the Chicago City Colleges since 1968. The author or coauthor of ten textbooks, he was named Distinguished Professor in 1991, Illinois Community College Trustees Association Teacher of the Year in 1991, and AAHH Exemplary Teacher in 1991. He has been Chair of the Communications Department of Harry S Truman College since 1990. His proudest accomplishments are his children, Sarah and Brad.

**Elizabeth Nist** was born in Philadelphia and grew up in Los Angeles. After graduating from Cal State Northridge, she began teaching at Moorpark Junior College in 1969. For eighteen years, she lived in Orem, Utah, where she taught at Utah Valley Community College and the University of Utah. Currently, she serves as the Online Curriculum Specialist at Anoka Ramsey Community College in Coon Rapids, Minnesota, where she has been teaching English since 1990. Her husband, Jack, teaches at North Hennepin Community College. They have three children and three grandchildren.

**Mary Slayter** lives in Grants Pass, Oregon, and recently retired from Rogue Community College where she taught for thirty years. She has served as a member of the Executive Committee of the Conference on College Composition and Communication and as chair of the National Two-Year College Council (now TYCA) of the National Council of Teachers of English. She received a Fulbright

Fellowship for study in Chile and was chosen to participate in an NEH seminar in classical archaeology in Greece.

**Barbara Stout** was a member of the English Department at the Rockville Campus of Montgomery College in Maryland from 1971 to 2001. She was chairperson of her department for ten years, secretary of the Conference on College Composition and Communication from 1995 to 1999, and active in the Two-Year College English Association. She is coauthor, with John Chaffee and Christine McMahon, of *Critical Thinking, Thoughtful Writing* and has contributed chapters on two-year-college English programs and writing-across-the-curriculum to NCTE, Jossey-Bass, and Sage publications.

**Howard Tinberg** is a Professor of English and Director of the Writing Lab at Bristol Community College, Massachusetts. He is the current editor of *Teaching English in the Two-Year College*, a journal published by the National Council of Teachers of English. He is the author of two books: *Border Talk: Writing and Knowing in the Two-Year College* (NCTE, 1997) and *Writing with Consequence: What Writing Does in the Disciplines* (Longman, 2003). He has published articles in a variety of journals, including *College English, College Composition and Communication, Teaching English in the Two-Year College,* and *Journal of Basic Writing*. He is currently working (with coauthor Patrick Sullivan) on a third book called *What Is College-Level Writing?* In 2004, he was named the Carnegie Foundation CASE Community College Professor of the Year.

**Richard Williamson** is Professor Emeritus of English and Film Production at the College of San Mateo in California. He is author (with Laura Hackett) of *Anatomy of Reading* and *Design for Composition*. His stories and articles have been published in numerous magazines and journals. These days, he divides his time between travel and writing about it.